¹Thing
ın

~~and follow his reading~~

Kimberly
Benjamin

"It's obvious that this book is inspired by the Holy Spirit. The way the Scriptures relate to each topic displays how this book truly lines up with the Word of God. I like how the book starts each chapter with a verse and ends with a prayer."

- Anthony Luckett
Professor, Macomb Community College

"I'm mad that this book wasn't out when I was unemployed. The tools and the principles used in this book are the ones I used on my job search. I really connected with the speaking what you want section because the current job I have now was literally spoken into existence and God really showed out on this job for my life. Awesome, awesome, awesome job. Keep up the good work."

- Maurice Lynch
Audio Visual Technician
University of Detroit Mercy School of Law

"*How to Be Highly Favored and Empowered to Prosper in Your Job Search* is truly a long overdue recipe for success in the stressful plight of finding employment. Kimberly has done an excellent job in making a user-friendly antidote that is Spirit-filled and guaranteed to help those in the need of employment assistance."

- Cathy McQuarters
Human Resources Supervisor
Daimler Chrysler Corporation

"Helping people to achieve greater heights is her goal. Seeing people excel in life is her passion. Serving the Lord by serving His people is her joy. Disclosed in this book are many treasures to help you become bold in your endeavors to be highly resourceful in your job search and learn more about yourself along the way. You walk away from this book feeling more confident in making decisions for today and for the future. Get to know Kimberly Benjamin by getting to know her work in this book and you will surely *Be Blessed*."

- Willie Bell
President and CEO
Advanced Freelance Inc.

HOW TO BE
HIGHLY
FAVORED
AND EMPOWERED TO
PROSPER
IN YOUR JOB SEARCH

PROVEN STRATEGIES FOR JOB SEARCH SUCCESS

KIMBERLY A. BENJAMIN, PHR

"Be Blessed" Career Consulting Inc.

How to Be Highly Favored and Empowered to Prosper in Your Job Search
Kimberly A. Benjamin

ISBN 0-9766785-0-0
Copyright © 2005
"Be Blessed" Career Consulting Inc.
P.O. Box 4373 Southfield, MI 48037
(586) 718-2571 E-mail: beblessedcc@aol.com
www.BeBlessedCareerConsulting.com

Library of Congress Control Number: 2005903910
1. Career Planning 2. Job Search 3. Personal Growth 4. Christian Life
5. Self-Help 6. Spiritual

"Be Blessed" Books are available at special quantity discounts to use as premiums and sales promotions, or for use in corporate training sessions. For more information, please write to Director of Sales, "Be Blessed" Career Consulting Inc. P.O. Box 4373 Southfield, MI 48037 or contact your local bookstore.

"Be Blessed" Career Consulting Inc. is licensed, bonded and required to operate in the State of Michigan and regulated by the department. "Be Blessed" Career Consulting Inc. is not an employment agency and is not permitted to schedule interviews or to in any way put you in direct contact with potential employers outside of providing lists of recruiters, agencies and job search headhunters. Advice given by "Be Blessed" Career Consulting Inc. representatives are provided as a service to the general public and does not assume liability for the actions of its readers.

Editorial: Michael Bryant, Stacey Hanks, Georgena Harrington and Kym Moore
Cover and Interior Design by LaTanya Orr-Terry, LTerry Design.
Printed by McNaughton & Gunn, Inc., Saline, MI

Lord,

I want to thank You for creating me. I thank You for placing inside my heart the desire to help others achieve their career goals. I am blessed because of Your never-ending love and I am grateful for the opportunity to tell the world about it through this book.

To God be the Glory Forever. Amen.

Dedication

This book is dedicated to every person that is looking for a new job and may have felt lost and discouraged. My prayer is that you find this book an uplifting and practical guide as you go through your job search.

With Christ, all things are possible to him that believes. Keep believing in Christ and the job of your dreams will manifest. Take this time to draw closer to God. Allow Him to strengthen, encourage, and minister to you during this important time in your life. Besides, He knows your future anyway. Trust Him.

TABLE OF CONTENTS

PART E: A Closer Look at "Be Blessed" Career Consulting Inc.

INTRODUCTION

There are many reasons why you should read this book. For starters, *"The blessing of the Lord, it maketh rich, and he addeth no sorrow with it"* (Proverbs 10:22). Everyone wants to be highly favored and empowered to prosper, but not everyone knows how to become victorious in that area.

I don't know about you, but I want to be in the Lord's will and complete happiness while going through my job search. Looking for a job doesn't have to be a struggle. It won't be if we do our part.

The last things that you want to do is move too fast and not seek God first about your next career move. He could want you to pursue another career field that will give you the opportunity to utilize the gifts, skills and talents that He gave you when He created you.

Many times, when people are looking for jobs, they tend to focus their search on similar positions that they had in the past. They don't consider that maybe, just maybe, God wants to do a "New Thing" in their lives that will bring them more joy and fulfillment.

> *"Remember ye not the former things, neither consider*
> *the things of old. Behold, I will do a new thing; now it shall*
> *spring forth; shall ye not know it? I will even make a way in*
> *the wilderness, and rivers in the desert."*
> *- Isaiah 43:18-19*

Perhaps the Lord has been training you to be in a higher position within your field of interest. Maybe the Lord wants you to spend this time attending to the needs of your family, or maybe this is the time that the Lord wants you to "step out on faith" and steward a business for the Kingdom of God. You will never know the answer to these questions until you spend time with God.

As stated before, *"The blessing of the Lord, it maketh rich, and addeth no sorrow with it"* (Proverbs 10:22). Would you like to be rich? Would you like to make more money in your next job? Many people say that they would like to make more money but don't really understand the steps needed to get them there. In this book, we will discuss the things that you will need to do to be highly favored over other candidates, be empowered to prosper by making more money, and be happier in your life. So grab a pen, your *How to Be Highly Favored and Empowered to Prosper in Your Job Search Workbook*, this book, and let's get started!

PART A

A Closer Look at Yourself

A New Beginning

"Remember ye not the former things, neither consider the things of old. Behold, I will do a new thing; now it shall spring forth; shall ye not know it? I will even make a way in the wilderness, and rivers in the desert."
— *Isaiah 43:18-19*

It's a new day. A new day begins with many things, . . the chirping of birds as they sing, . . the sun rising to welcome us with light and heat, . . the wind blowing gently against our face. A new day can be a tremendous blessing if you allow it to be in your life!

Just because you may have lost your job, it doesn't mean that this is the end of the world. Have you stopped to consider that this opportunity is a blessing for you? Many times people spend a lot of time being busy and forget to be thankful in their current state. We are always rushing to get to a new destination. When was the last time you just sat quietly in a park, in your backyard, or in your car with the sole purpose of relaxing and listening to God? He is always with us, waiting for us to acknowledge Him and His presence.

3

No matter the reason why you are currently looking for employment, the bottom line is that you are here, and that you are not alone. You have another chance to do something that you desire. Remember that God will be with you always even until the end of the world (Matthew 28:20).

What are you going to do with this opportunity that has been given to you today? Are you going to revert back to looking for a job that you don't enjoy or are you going to take the "new day" that God has given you to slow down and spend time in His Word so that He can speak to you about the career that you should pursue?

> "In the beginning God created the heaven and the earth.
> And the earth was without form, and void; and darkness
> was upon the face of the deep. And the Spirit of God moved
> upon the face of the waters. And God said,
> Let there be light: and there was light."
> - Genesis 1:1-3

As you can see in Genesis 1:1-3, God speaks things into existence. God has also equipped us with that same ability as believers. What has He been saying to you about your job purpose? What skills and talents has He equipped you with to share with others? What are the activities and things that bring you joy and peace? What is that job that you know you should be doing but you haven't pursued?

Take some time today to slow down and let God minister to you about your career and purpose in life. Who knows . . . He may be giving you a wonderful opportunity to start your career as a new beginning.

Take this time to listen to God. I believe that God is always trying to speak to us, but sometimes we are too busy to hear His voice. I don't know about you, but I want to make sure that I spend time with Him to know His voice.

> *"Blessed is the man that heareth me, watching daily at my gates,*
> *waiting at the posts of my doors. For whoso findeth me*
> *findeth life, and shall obtain favour of the Lord."*
> *- Proverbs 8:34-35*

> *"Blessed are they that do his commandments..."*
> *- Revelation 22:14*

It is very important to do what God instructs you to do in order to
be blessed by God. Trusting in God will lead you to peace. Peace
is priceless. You may have a lot of money, treasures, and friends in
your life; however, if peace isn't present, confusion and fear will step
in and rob you of the blessing.

Keep in mind that God will only bless what He is doing. So it is
extremely important to be able to hear from God in your job search.
When you spend more time with God, you are able to hear His
voice clearly and make better decisions about your career.

Personal Assignments

1. Spend some time with God today. Go to a park, your backyard,
   your car, or anywhere quiet to let Him minister to you about
   your purpose and the career that you should be pursuing.

2. Purchase the ***How to Be Highly Favored and Empowered to
   Prosper in Your Job Search Workbook*** to write down everything
   that God reveals to you during your job search.

3. Go to the Public Library, or surf the Internet, to locate information about the career of interest that was revealed to you
   during your personal time with God. Ask the librarian for
   assitance if needed.

4. Identify the kinds of training, education, licenses, or skills that you will need to receive to enter the profession identified.

5. Make plans to receive the training needed for your career of interest.

Prayer

Thank You Lord for my new beginning. Help me to slow down and hear from You regarding every step that You want me to pursue in my career. Even though I may not understand why I am in this new phase of life, I trust in You and Your Word. You will be with me always. I dedicate my job search to You. Amen.

Your Personal Self-Assessment

Chapter Two

"Examine yourselves, whether ye be in the faith;
prove your ownselves . . ."
- 2 Corinthians 13:5

This chapter is designed for you to do some inner reflecting about your past behavior and your personal career goals. In order for us to truly develop, we must understand the areas that we need to improve. Please take a moment to answer the following questions:

Select two statements that sound the most like you . . .

( ) Perceives, recognizes, and distinguishes the difference between right and wrong.

( ) Performs practical needs, and spends time in service to help others.

( ) Disseminates and manages information. Teaching. Researching.

(   ) Desires to make the lives of people more successful, encourage and build up.

(   ) Mobilizes resources for the aid and benefit of others.

(   ) Facilitates, organizes, and administrates.

(   ) Attends and cares for the emotional needs of others.

+ What is the date that you officially started your job search?
+ What date would you like to be in your new position?
+ What is the date that you will consider working outside of your preferred career?
+ Why are you currently looking for employment?
+ What resources have you used to assist with your job search? (ex: recruiters, job headhunters, employment agencies, newspaper, Internet, job fairs, networking, job hot lines, phone book, etc.)
+ Do you have a professionally created cover letter and résumé?
+ Is your résumé current?
+ Do you have a thank you letter created?
+ What were some of your past jobs?
+ What did you like least about each job you listed above?
+ What did you like most about each job you listed above?
+ What would you have changed about each job you listed above?
+ Which job listed would you have kept even if you didn't get paid for doing it?
+ How was your relationship with your past supervisors?
+ What made the relationship with one of your supervisors successful? What did you do? What did you learn?
+ What should you have done to make the relationship with a past supervisor more successful?

✦ What do you enjoy doing in your spare time?

✦ What talents and skills have you been blessed with by the Lord?

✦ What telephone number is best for a company to call you during your job search? Is this number on your résumé and cover letter?

✦ When is the best time for a company to call you?

✦ What is the minimum pay rate or salary base that you will accept?

✦ What is the maximum pay rate or salary base you will accept?

✦ What is your current mailing address? Is it on your cover letter and résumé?

✦ What is your current E-mail address? Is it on your cover letter and résumé?

✦ What was your least favorite job? Why?

✦ What kind of company do you want to work for? Why?

✦ Do you like working for a small, midsize, or large company? Why?

✦ What is more important to you: A high starting salary, personal career growth, or career advancement? Why?

✦ How far would you commute to work on a daily basis?

✦ How much travel would you consider doing on a weekly basis? 15 percent, 25 percent, 50 percent or 75 percent?

✦ Would you relocate to another state? If so, where?

✦ Do you like working in a small or a large department? Why?

✦ What industry would you like to work in? (ex: service, technology, manufacturing, etc.)

✦ How often would you like to receive a performance review from your supervisor?

✦ What kind of environment do you prefer working in? (ex: office, plant, outdoors, etc.)

✦ What were the relationships with your past co-workers? What did you learn about yourself?

✦ What is your ideal job or dream job?

✦ Do you have letters of recommendation from past co-workers and supervisors from each previous job? If so, list their name and phone numbers.

✦ Do you have a list of professional references to use during your job search? If so, list their names, phone numbers, job titles, and company names.

✦ Do you have a list of personal references to use during your job search?

✦ What equipment do you know how to operate? List them.

✦ What software do you know how to use? List them.

✦ What training course have you completed? List course title and year completed.

✦ What areas would you like to receive additional training?

✦ What professional organizations or associations have you been a member of? List name and year participated.

✦ What licenses or certifications have you received? Include year.

✦ What honors or awards have you received? Include month and year.

✦ Have you been involved in the community? If so, list organization name, program, and year participated.

✦ Would you rather work for a unionized or non-unionized company?

✦ What university, college, or trade school classes have you completed? List school, program name along with each class completed.

✦ Where would you like to see yourself in 3-5 years?

✦ Where would you like to see yourself in 8-10 years?

✦ What are your career goals? What will you do to obtain them?

✦ What are 10 of your personal goals? What will you do to obtain them?

✦ Why did you leave your last seven jobs? List reason for each job change.

✦ Do you believe that your current or last job is in the field that you should pursue at this time in your life? Why or why not?

✦ What is the highest level of education you have completed to date?

✦ Would you consider returning to school? If so, in what program would you enroll?

✦ Did you receive your high school diploma/GED? If not, do you plan on returning to school to receive it?

✦ Are you currently working on obtaining a degree, license, or certification? If so, list them.

✦ What are some responsibilities that you would like to have in your dream job?

✦ What are the areas that you will need to develop in order to be qualified for your dream job?

✦ What are your strengths?

✦ What areas do you need to improve in?

✦ What are your strong selling points?

✦ What areas do you have experience in?

✦ What is your job title with your current employer?

✦ What are the names of your past/current company competitors? List them.

✦ What companies would you like to work for in the future? List company name, address, and phone number.

✦ Are you happy with your current salary?

✦ Do you have access to the Internet?

✦ Do you have an E-mail address?

✦ Do you know how to use Microsoft Word?

✦ Do you have a fax number?

✦ Do you have a professional sounding message on your voicE-mail?

✦ Do you have networking/business cards to distribute to contacts during your job search?

✦ What will need to happen that will allow you to know that your job search was successful?

PERSONAL ASSIGNMENTS

1. Read all questions listed in this chapter.

2. Log the answers to the above listed questions in your *How to Be Highly Favored and Empowered to Prosper in Your Job Search Workbook.*

3. Contact "Be Blessed" Career Consulting Inc. to receive a FREE cover letter and résumé evaluation at:
   P.O. Box 4373, Southfield, Michigan 48037
   Call (586) 718-2571
   E-mail: Beblessedcc@aol.com, or log on to
   www.BeBlessedCareerConsulting.com.

Prayer

Lord, thank You for revealing to me the areas in my life that I need to work on. Thank You for allowing me to work for various companies in my past where my skills and abilities had an opportunity to develop. Help me to remember the areas that I need to improve in now in order for me to have a successful career transition. Amen.

WHERE IS YOUR CONFIDENCE?

CHAPTER THREE

*"It is better to trust in the LORD than to
put confidence in man."*
- Psalm 118:8

I t is very easy to become discouraged after losing a job and
forget who you are in Christ. Many people may tie their self
worth to a career, company, or job title. After reading this
chapter, you will learn to put your confidence in the Lord.

I remember how good it felt working for a major automotive
company in the Detroit, Michigan area. I thought that I had "finally
arrived" at the place in my career that I had been searching for. My
mother had worked for this company almost her entire life, and I
felt that I could now continue that tradition. Ultimately, I hoped
that I could retire from the same organization later on in my life. I
remember walking through the headquarters thinking about how
proud I had made my mother. I thought I would work there for
years and move up through the ranks. I didn't pay attention to how
the corporate atmosphere had changed. I started to hear about

budget cuts and cost controls. I didn't pay attention to how isolated I felt with the team that I worked on since I was new to the group.

One day I was called into a meeting in a conference room at 4:45 PM on a Friday. I felt that something was wrong, because I knew that meetings normally did not start late on a Friday. I sat down and in walked my supervisor and her boss. I sat patiently as they shared with me the reasons why they were going to have to let me go. At that time, all of the signs that I missed earlier that year came to me and the picture was clear. I couldn't believe that I was being "Let Go," but I was. I thanked my supervisor and her boss for allowing me the opportunity to work for them and I picked up my pad of paper and left the room.

As I went to my cubicle I began to think about how God could be glorified from this experience. I didn't want the devil to think that he won in this situation so I placed one of my praise and worship CDs in my computer and began to praise God as I packed up my belongings. I still remember seeing my supervisors' boss staring at me with amazement as I praised God after being let go from this major company. I learned a valuable lesson through that experience. Always place your confidence in the Lord Jesus Christ. Not in ourselves, or in companies.

Personal Assignments

1. Take a moment to reflect on why and how you left your past places of employment. Was it by your choice or your employer's?

2. Were there any signals that you saw, heard, or received but overlooked? What came to your remembrance?

3. Consider your last place of employment. What should you have done to improve your work performance?

4. How would you act if you were confident that God would take care of your needs?

5. List things in your *How to Be Highly Favored and Empowered to Prosper in Your Job Search Workbook* that have been revealed to you by God about your past work experience.

6. Make a list of "I Will Do" and "I Won't Do" at your next place of employment.

Prayer

Lord, please forgive me for my past negative behaviors demonstrated at my previous places of employment. Please forgive me for holding on to anger and unforgiveness towards any previous employer. Even though I may not understand why I lost my job, I trust You to make a way for me. I put my confidence and trust in You. Amen.

NETWORKING:
HAVE YOU ENTERTAINED
AN ANGEL UNAWARES?

CHAPTER • FOUR

*"Be not forgetful to entertain strangers: for thereby
some have entertained angels unawares."*
- Hebrews 13:2

I am deeply troubled when I meet job seekers that do not like to network with others while they are looking for a new job. I realize that some of you don't like to let people know that you are unemployed and need assistance with locating employment. I would like to challenge you by asking this simple question: How can people help you if you don't tell them what you need?

Some of you may feel vulnerable and don't like to ask people for help. Others let pride get in the way. My advice to you is . . . Get over it!!! Stop feeling sorry about your situation and let God send people across your path to bless you. Remember, the Lord uses people to bless others and get things done here in the earth. You may have very well walked by angels unaware in your job search. You could have by-passed friends, family members, co-workers, professional club members, colleagues, recruiters, business owners, hiring managers, or even actual angels, that were looking for a person like you to fill a position in their company.

The scripture in Hebrews 13:2 remains true. God has sent many people your way to minister to you as well as bless you. Open your mouth and let people know that you need assistance. You can turn your situation around now by completing the personal assignments listed below. It is never too late to start networking with others. So get busy!

Personal Assignments

1. Go to a quiet place where you are alone. List 50 people that currently know that you are looking for employment. Follow-up with them to see if they have any job leads for you.

2. List 100 people that you know. List everyone that comes to your mind. List friends, family members, old supervisors, co-workers, vendors, past company competitors, neighbors, club members, past clients and customers, teachers, ministers, suppliers, friends of your family members, and professional organization and association members.

3. Split your list in half. Identify the first 50 people that you will contact this month. Identify the next 50 people that you will contact next month.

4. Send a copy of your résumé to all 100 of your contacts identified in the brainstorming exercise listed above (via mail, fax, or E-mail).

5. Write a 30-second script that you will use as you call the selected contacts listed above. The script should include the following components: Your name, the purpose of the call, your positions

of interest, what you are asking them to do for you, your phone number, and the best time that they can reach you.

Prayer

*Lord, I just want to thank You for the ministering angels that
You have sent forth to assist me with my job search. I thank You
for the people that are praying for me and standing in faith with me for
the right job that You have for me, that will manifest in due season.*

*I thank You for the boldness to speak to others and request help.
I thank You for Your love and provisions. My confidence is in You.*

*Thanks in advance for giving me the words to say when I
network with others this week. I am led by You. I will know
when to speak, what to say, and how to say it. Thank You for
ordering my steps and for all of the "Divine Appointments"
that You have in store for me. Amen.*

Interviewing:
And With All Thy Getting,
Get Understanding

CHAPTER FIVE

*"Wisdom is the principal thing; therefore get wisdom:
and with all thy getting get understanding. Exalt her, and
she shall promote thee: she shall bring thee honour,
when thou dost embrace her."*
- Proverbs 4:7-8

The telephone is a valuable tool in today's job search. It can be used for networking and contacting employers. According to an article in the *Bernard Haldane News*, many job hunters misinterpret receiving a phone call, as opposed to a letter, as a lack of interest. Instead, these "screening calls" frequently mean that the résumé has sparked an employer's curiosity. The company simply wants more information before committing to a face-to-face interview.

As you can see, having the proper skills to be able to effectively communicate on the telephone is essential. Many recruiters will allow you to reschedule a phone interview if you are not ready for the call; however, some recruiters will consider it a strike against you if you are not willing to take their call at the time it was placed. They will simply move on to the next candidate on their list.

The following are four reasons why human resource professionals are conducting more telephone interviews today:
- To pre-screen applicants.
- To reduce their travel expense.
- The ability to interview more candidates.
- Allows global staff to participate in the interview.

The following are tips on how to successfully execute a telephone interview:
- Have a self-confident and enthusiastic voice.
- Be concise and to the point with your examples. Do not be long winded.
- Avoid "Yes" or "No" answers. Give important details, but don't be long winded.
- Be in a comfortable and quiet place to take the interview.
- Don't eat, drink, or chew gum while interviewing.
- Speak directly into the phone.
- Get the name and phone number of the interviewer just in case the phone call is dropped.
- If you are in your car when you receive the call, pull over to a safe and quiet place.
- Take notes for future use.
- Keep your job search materials in a convenient location (portable folder or binder) so in case you get an unexpected phone call you can get to them quickly.
- Have the job description, if applicable, your cover letter and résumé and company notes in front of you for easy reference.
- Practice mock telephone interviews with a friend.
- Have a professional sounding answering machine message. Music should not be playing in the background.
- Be friendly and polite to the interviewer.
- Remember to ask the interviewer 4-8 questions.

✦ Get the name, title, address, and phone number of the interviewer so that you can send them a thank you letter.

✦ Make sure you have the proper spelling of their full name.

✦ Thank the caller for taking the time to conduct the interview.

✦ Restate your interest in the position and that you look forward to meeting the interviewer and his/her staff in person.

✦ Do not share your salary goals with the interviewer at this time. When asked about your desired salary, just state that you are "open" and "flexible" and look forward to learning more about the position to ensure a good fit.

CONFIDENCE IN GOD

In order for you to be comfortable and confident while being interviewed you must remember that the Lord is with you always (Mathew 28:20). Many people may not particularly care for being interviewed, but this step is necessary in order to ensure that the right person is selected for the job.

It is your responsibility to let the interviewer know that you are the "Right Person" for the job. It is also important that you do your best in the interview and project a professional and confident image. A great way to prepare for a successful interview is to practice responding to the following commonly asked interview questions:

✦ Why do you want to work for this company?
✦ Why should I hire you for this position?
✦ What are your strengths and weaknesses?
✦ What do you know about our company?

✦ Why are you looking to leave your current employer?

✦ How did you handle a difficult situation in the past?

✦ How much money are you looking for?

✦ How much money do you currently make a year?

✦ How long have you been looking for employment?

✦ Why did you leave your last 4 employers?

✦ What are your short term and long term career goals?

✦ Why did you choose your major?

✦ How did you lead a team in the past? Provide examples.

✦ How did you handle working with a difficult boss? Provide examples.

✦ How did you work with others on your team? Provide examples. What was your role?

✦ In this position the person will make around $20,000 a year. Is this okay with you?

✦ Would you be willing to take a drug test?

✦ May I contact your current employer to conduct a reference check?

✦ What are your two greatest work achievements?

✦ How did you handle making easy decisions? Provide an example.

✦ Are you willing to relocate to another state? If so, where?

✦ What were your favorite subjects in school and why?

✦ Do you prefer working in a team or independently?

✦ When are you available to begin work?

✦ I've noticed on your résumé that there are gaps in your dates of employment. What were you doing during this time?

✦ What skills do you need to improve upon?

✦ This job requires a lot of travel; will this be a problem with you?

✦ How many hours are you willing to work during the week?

+ What was the most difficult experience that you had with an employer? How did you handle it?

BEHAVIORAL INTERVIEWS

As a human resource professional with over 13 years of experience in the field, I can tell you that a recruiter is trained to listen closely to each applicants' response to their specific questions to evaluate their decision making capabilities. A candidate should be able to think on their feet, answer all questions directly and in a professional manner. When being asked behavioral interview questions based on your past or current working experience, you should remember the following five steps:

+ Identify the name or type of project that you worked on that is an excellent example of your work, and showcases your skills and abilities.
+ Highlight the role you played in completing the project or resolving the problem.
+ List the key steps that you took to complete the project or resolve the problem.
+ Identify the outcome and your role in its completion.
+ Identify how the completion of your project impacted the company bottom line (ex: saved company money, reduced cost, improved processes, lowered overhead cost, increased customer satisfaction, improved employee morale, increased customer base, improved productivity, decreased part defects, etc.).

QUESTIONS TO ASK YOURSELF ABOUT YOUR PREVIOUS INTERVIEWS

+ When was the last time you were interviewed?
+ What can you recall about the interview?

✦ How did you prepare for the interview?
✦ What areas do you feel you need to improve in the interviewing process?
✦ Did you compare your résumé with the job posting?
✦ How many people interviewed you?
✦ How did you obtain information about the company and position?
✦ Did you ask 4-8 questions during the interview?
✦ Do you like to be interviewed? Why or why not?
✦ Did you ask for a business card for all interviews met?

THINGS TO DO BEFORE THE FACE-TO-FACE INTERVIEW

✦ Pray to God, thanking Him for the interview and ask Him for wisdom to answer the questions properly.
✦ Arrive at the interview location 30 minutes early.
✦ Spend 15 minutes in your car reviewing the company literature and job posting material.
✦ Select 6-10 important projects or experiences included on your résumé that demonstrate that you are qualified for the job.
✦ Research the company history, current performance, and future goals.
✦ Ask three people to interview you to help improve your interviewing skills. Review their feedback.
✦ Identify 4-8 questions that you would like to ask the recruiter during the interview.
✦ Eat a good breakfast while still in your pajamas. Do not wear your interview clothes to avoid getting them dirty.
✦ Get a good nights' sleep the day before.
✦ Drive to the location where the interview will be conducted two days before the scheduled date to test the route.

✦ Make a list of your key accomplishments.

✦ Decide on the outfit that you will wear to the interview three days in advance. Ensure the outfit is clean and neatly pressed. Many businesses now have a dress code of business casual. You should always lean more on the business side rather than casual for interviews. Conservative suits are always safe and exhibit professionalism. The preferred colors to wear to an interview are navy blue, black, and gray.

✦ Place a notepad in your briefcase for note taking during the interview.

✦ Polish your shoes and briefcase the night before.

✦ Bring extra copies of your résumé and list of references to give to the interviewer(s).

✦ Create a business portfolio that displays your résumé, list of references, letters of recommendation, educational transcripts, training certificates, awards, work samples, diplomas, degrees, professional membership documentation, published work, scholarships, thank you letters, recognition of accomplishments, software proficiency, creative projects, special skill listing, presentations, professional qualifications, licenses, and language proficiency. Bringing a portfolio with you to your interview will allow you to stand out among the other candidates. Contact Be Blessed Career Consulting Inc. at www.BeBlessedCareerConsulting.com or (586) 718-2571 to get a professional business portfolio created to use during your job search.

✦ Remove nose, eyebrow, and tongue earrings.

✦ Cover all body tattoos.

✦ For men - remove all earrings (this will help the interviewer to focus on your skills and abilities instead of your appearance).

✦ For women - wear small earrings no larger than the size

of a penny. Only wear one pair of earrings if you have
multiple holes.

✦ Do not wear clunky and noisy jewelry.

✦ Wear very little perfume or cologne
(the interviewer may be allergic to your scent).

✦ Wear only clear fingernail polish to draw the interviewers
attention away from your fingernails.

✦ Make sure your hygiene is clean (ex: take a shower, brush
your teeth, do not smoke, and use deodorant).

✦ Bring personal and professional reference contact
information (name, title, address, phone number) just in
case you need to fill out an employment application.

✦ Thank God for the opportunity to meet with the
recruiter and praise Him ahead of time for a successful
interview.

THINGS TO DO DURING THE INTERVIEW

✦ Bring extra copies of your résumé to give to the
interviewers.

✦ Ask the interviewer if you can place a copy of your
résumé on the desk in front of you. This will help you to
easily identify key experiences that you can share with
them during the interview process.

✦ Listen closely to each question the interviewer gives you
and ask for clarification for difficult questions when
needed.

✦ Ask the interviewer if you can take notes during the
process.

✦ Be calm and confident.

✦ Be enthusiastic about the position.

✦ Speak clearly.

+ Do not discuss money issues until you have been offered the job.
+ Answer negative questions and topics with positive points of view.
+ Listen, Talk, Listen, Talk, Talk, Talk. They have to get to know you and make sure that you are a great fit for the company. Clearly articulate why you are the best fit. Nod your head and provide non-verbal feedback to the interviewer.
+ Ask the interviewer 4-8 questions during the interview.
+ Request a business card from each interviewer.
+ Look the interviewer in the eye, give a firm handshake, and then restate your interest in the position.

THINGS TO DO AND QUESTIONS TO ASK YOURSELF AFTER EACH INTERVIEW

+ Send each interviewer a thank you letter within three days of the interview.
+ Reflect on the interview and evaluate yourself on how you answered each question.
+ What were your thoughts about the position? Will you accept the job offer if it was extended to you?
+ Write down the questions that you feel you didn't answer properly. Think of ways that you could improve the response for future interviews.
+ What are the next steps in the interviewing process?
+ Did you provide powerful work related experiences for each question asked?
+ Did you ask the interviewer questions? If so, how many? What were the questions asked? What were the responses?
+ Did you do most of the talking during the interview?
+ Did you answer each question directly and completely?

✦ Did you understand each question that the interviewer asked? Did you ask for clarification for the questions that were unclear?

PERSONAL ASSIGNMENTS

1. Go to a public library to research a company that interests you.

2. Purchase a binder to store job and company information.

3. Invest in an answering machine. Record a professional sounding outgoing message that does not have music playing in the background.

4. Practice mock job interviews with a friend. Allow them to ask you 30 questions. Ask them 4-8 questions at the end of the interview.

5. Select five outfits that you will wear to interviews this year. Try on all five outfits and have six professional people evaluate you on your appearance. Make changes as recommended.

6. Contact "Be Blessed" Career Consulting Inc. to schedule a personalized consultation to help develop your Business Portfolio and professional interview attire.

Prayer

Thank You Lord for the many interviews that You have lined up for me. Thank You for allowing the interviewers to see Your character through me. I know that You will be with me in each interview that I participate in this year. I will answer each question asked correctly and I will ask the right questions during the interview. Lord, I will not be nervous but I will be confident during the interview. Thank You in advance that the interviewers will feel comfortable in my presence and receive knowledge from You as to how I can be a valuable asset to their company. Thank You for also revealing to me the correct job that You want me to have. Amen.

Part B

A Closer Look at Character Traits Needed for a Successful Job Search

DILIGENCE

"Wherefore the rather, brethren, give diligence to make your calling and election sure: for if ye do these things, ye shall never fall."
- 2 Peter 1:10

Looking for a job takes more than just skill; it takes a good character. Too often job seekers think that if they fill out an employment application, apply for a job posting, or just send in their résumé and cover letter to an employer, they have done their part. Don't be naive! It takes a good deal more than filling out a couple of forms to secure a job in today's job market. It also takes strong character.

So what is character? *The Character Training Institute* defines character as, "The qualities built into an individual's life that determine his or her response regardless of circumstances."

In this book, we have identified 12 character qualities that a job seeker should demonstrate successfully during their daily job search. Lets walk through each character quality together to get a better understanding of why they were selected. Let's start with diligence.

Diligence is defined as, "Investing my time and energy to complete each task assigned to me" (Character First, 2004). Looking for a job can be a lot of work and it is very important not to give up. You must be able to get up every morning with renewed strength to tackle another day.

Even though you may not have received a job offer today, it doesn't mean that the leads you get tomorrow won't be successful. Remember, God has no limits. You must be diligent in your daily job search, exhibiting a high level of commitment and energy to every assignment. You must believe that God will renew your strength during your job search.

Personal Assignments

1. Get up at 6:00 a.m. every day this week to spend time with God.

2. Work out for 30 minutes a day this week. (ex: fitness club, home, park, or neighborhood).

3. Go to the public library three days this week to conduct research as part of your job search. Ask the librarian for resources available that can help you locate employment.

Prayer

Lord, thank You for giving me the strength to be diligent.
I will be persistent in my daily efforts to look for employment.
I will get up early this week and spend time with You in Your Word.
I will spend some time this week to care for my body and health
by working out for 30 minutes a day. Thank You for giving me
the strength to complete all of my assignments. I know that with
You all things are possible; therefore, it is possible for me to
be diligent and complete everything that I said I would do
this week. Amen.

RESOURCEFULNESS

CHAPTER SEVEN

"For I, the LORD thy God, will hold thy right hand,
saying unto thee, fear not; I will help thee."
- Isaiah 41:13

For many of you, this may be the first time that you have had to look for employment as a result of corporate downsizing. Others of you may be a little bit more familiar with the process of looking for a job. The important thing to remember about both situations is that a change has occurred in your life and that you must be comfortable in utilizing different kinds of resources in order to have a successful job search. God could be doing a new thing in your life and you should trust in Him and His resources.

Resourcefulness is defined as, to be able to, *"Deal promptly and effectively with new situations, difficulties and problems; clever in finding resources,"*(Random House Unabridged Dictionary, 1997). How have you dealt with your new situation? Have you accepted the fact that God is doing a new thing in your life? Do you believe that God will provide resources for you during your job search?

One day you may need to look in the Sunday Newspaper Classified Section for a job. Another day you may need to apply for a job by using the telephone or Internet. On another day you may need to contact employment agencies for job leads. Regrettably, many times job seekers focus strictly on obtaining a "permanent" job and forget to consider other resources that God has available for them.

When I first began my job search, after losing my job, I had only considered applying for full-time "permanent" positions. After five months in my job search I was presented with an opportunity to interview for a "contract" position through an agency for a large company in my field of interest. Initially, I did not consider applying for the position because it wasn't a so-called "permanent" job. Once I let down my boundaries, and thanked God for providing me with His valuable resource, I was able to look at the job for what it was . . . "A Blessing from God," and accepted the position once an offer was made.

I have now been with the same company for over four years, doing what I love. The Lord has blessed me with unspeakable favor with this job that no amount of money could ever fully compensate for. Remember, God is your source. So let Him bring you new resources to help with your job search.

PERSONAL ASSIGNMENTS

1. Identify resources that you have used in the past to assist you in your current job search.

2. Look in the newspaper at the jobs that you are not interested in. What is the name of the company that is advertising the position? Send your résumé to the companies listed that you have an interest in pursuing.

3. List 20 companies that you have an interest in working for in the future. Visit the company web-site for each company listed above. Visit their job posting section on their Web site to see if they have any job openings.

4. Identify 10 company telephone hotline numbers to call to inquire about employment.

5. Call your local television station to see if they are aware of any job openings in the community.

6. Look in the telephone book to identify 10 temporary agencies. Call each agency selected to inquire about open positions with their clients.

7. Identify industry trade journals, professional organizations and associations that are in your field of interest. Contact the resources identified to see if they have open positions in your areas of interest.

Prayer

Lord, thank You for providing resources for me. You always make a way out of no way, and I just want to thank You for it. Thank You for sending people my way to bless me this week. Thank You for helping me to realize that there are a lot of resources available to me. Help me to identify other valuable resources that You would like me to use during my job search. You are my source, therefore, You will provide the resources for me to use. I just want to thank You in advance for a successful job search! Amen.

SELF-CONTROL

CHAPTER EIGHT

"Let your moderation be known unto all men. The Lord is at hand."
- Philippians 4:5

S elf-control is defined as, *"The restraint exercised over oneself or over one's own emotions, desires, actions, or impulses,"* (Character First Bulletins, 2002). It is very important that you demonstrate self-control during your job search. It is important to use your time and resources wisely.

SELF-CONTROL IN YOUR PERSONAL LIFE

It can be very easy to become lazy during your job search because of the perceived amount of "free time" that's available to you. The saying, . . "It is a job, looking for a job," is still very true. It is extremely important to have a daily game plan, and to put together a schedule to utilize your time effectively. I recommend getting up early in the morning (preferably around 6:00 a.m.) so that you can spend time praying and meditating on the Word of God before you begin your job search.

SELF-CONTROL IN YOUR FINANCES

Another important area that demands self-control during your job search is that of your finances. It is very important that you have money in your savings account dedicated to your job search. If you are not wise the money that you saved will be depleted quickly.

Put God in your personal finances and allow Him to minister to you about what you should do with your money. Remember, all of the money that you have is His and you should manage it properly. The ultimate goal is to have the Lord say unto you, "Well done, thou good and faithful servant: thou hast been faithful over a few things, I will make thee ruler over many things: enter thou into the joy of thy lord" (Matthew 25:21).

When you are able to manage your finances with what is available to you (even if it does not appear to be much), you show the Lord that He can trust you and bless you with more money in the future. So show God that you can have self-control and be faithful with what He has already given you.

PERSONAL ASSIGNMENTS

1. Create a budget that monitors the amount of money that you are taking in and spending during your job search.

2. Keep copies of the receipts for items that you've purchased during your job search.

3. Add up your expenses at the end of the month. What have you learned about your spending pattern?

4. Identify things that you will cut back on this month.

5. Balance your checkbook weekly.

6. Identify the amount of money that you will have dedicated for your job search.

7. Create a schedule that you will use Monday - Friday (in 30 minute increments) starting at 6:00 a.m. and ending around 7:00 p.m. to use during your job search. List tasks that you will complete daily to ensure that you have a successful job search.

Prayer

Thank You Lord for providing me with self-control in my personal life and finances. Reveal to me in my life the areas I need to demonstrate more self-control. Help me to create a plan and stick to it. I will get up early and spend time with You in Your Word. I will only purchase things from this day forward that are in my budget. I will demonstrate to You in my job search and in my finances that I can be faithful over the little things so that You can make me ruler over much. For that I thank You. Amen.

BOLDNESS

CHAPTER NINE

*"In whom we have boldness and access with
confidence by the faith of him."*
- Ephesians 3:12

A re you courageous and daring, not hesitant, or not fearful in the face of possible or present danger? Well, if you answered "Yes" then you are a person that can demonstrate boldness during your job search.

"For God hath not given us the spirit of fear; but of power, and of love, and of a sound mind." (2 Timothy 1:7) There will be times in your job search when you will have to demonstrate the character quality of "boldness." You may need to call 100 companies to see if they are hiring. You may need to "hit the pavement," and actually visit companies to fill out employment applications. You may need to "follow-up" with past companies and resources that you've used to apply for open positions. Whatever the case, looking for a job requires that you operate in "Boldness."

I know that initiating contact with companies may be a little uncomfortable, but what other choice do you have? Initiating the first contact with an employer is critical because not all open jobs are advertised. Many career consulting experts in the field call this process "tapping into the hidden job market." According to studies by a major foundation and the Federal Employment Services in California, over 85 percent of job vacancies are not available through traditional resources like newspaper ads, civil service notices, federal or state employment agencies, private agencies or search firms. This tells us that job seekers must feel comfortable in initiating contact with the potential employer and find out about job openings before they are advertised.

As an experienced human resource professional, I have heard many complaints about positions being filled by family members, friends, and other preferred candidates before the position "officially" became available. Even though this process seems unfair, it is very true. I am not saying that the majority of companies have family members and friends working in the same organization, but that a large number of open positions were filled by "preferred candidates" that have submitted their résumé early in the job search process.

Many of the candidates have networked with key decision makers before the job posting was advertised to the general public. Millions of job hunters shop the local classifieds weekly without realizing that each ad for most openings draws hundreds of applicants. Also, jobs advertised in papers today only account for less than 3 percent of the jobs out there.

As you can see, it is very important that you send your cover letter and résumé to everyone that you come in contact with, such as recruiters, company vice presidents, executives, friends, and family members, early in the job search process. Applying for jobs that are ONLY advertised (ex: Sunday newspaper Classified Section, Internet job postings, and employment publications) limits your opportunities for God to provide resources to you.

Personal Assignments

1. How can you demonstrate boldness this week?

2. Identify 20 companies that you will call this week to inquire about open positions within the organization.

3. Identify 15 companies that you will call this week to schedule interviews.

4. Send your résumé to 15 local temporary or employment agencies.

Prayer

Lord, I thank You for boldness as I go through my job search.
I will be comfortable in speaking with friends, family members,
recruiters and potential employers about my employment needs.
Thank You for giving me the words to say as I network with others.
I am strong and confident because of You, and I thank You for letting
the recruiters see it in me throughout my job search. Amen.

EXCELLENCE

CHAPTER TEN

"Let them praise the name of the Lord: for his
name alone is excellent."
- Psalm 148:13

Excellence is defined as, *"An excellent quality or capacity,"* (Webster's New Riverside Dictionary, 1996). We should represent God in everything we do. Our conversation, behavior, dress, character and even résumé should be about excellence. What does your cover letter and résumé say about you?

Your cover letter and résumé are the first impression you give to a prospective employer. They reflect your skills, abilities, grammar, and professionalism. Their purpose is to get you the interview with the employer. Your cover letter and résumé must be neat, easy to read, pleasant to the eye, and error free. Both documents should also highlight your strengths, character, and personal accomplishments as it relates to the job you are interested in.

The Cover Letter

The purpose of a cover letter is to create a really good impression about you by highlighting your skills and accomplishments in a clear, concise manner. The cover letter actually "covers" the résumé. This is how it got its name. Cover letters are normally used when you present your résumé to a prospective employer without an initial interview. The cover letter helps the interviewer to quickly identify key skills and accomplishments within the first 15 seconds of scanning the résumé with an eye to reviewing the résumé again later. The following are some important things to keep in mind when you create a cover letter:

• Identify how you qualify for the position.
• State how you found out about the open position.
• Highlight your key accomplishments.
• Identify how they can reach you.
• Identify a time when you will contact them for follow-up.
• Ensure the cover letter is one page in length.
• Ensure the envelope matches your cover letter and résumé paper.
• Proofread your cover letter for errors.

The Résumé

The purpose of a résumé is to highlight your skills and accomplishments in a clear and concise manner as a prelude to getting a job interview. There are two kinds of résumés that a person can use during their job search. They are called, "Chronological" and "Functional." Chronological résumés should be used when you want to highlight your past work experience from your most recent employer down to your 1st employer. This style works particularly well when you want to highlight your valuable experience with past employers.

It is best to use a "Functional" résumé style when you desire to switch career fields. With this style you seek to highlight transferable skills that you received instead of work experience in a field you no longer wish to pursue. Common categories often used in functional résumés are: *Summary of Qualifications, Managerial and Supervisory, Customer Service, Marketing and Sales, Financial Record Keeping, Management, Interpersonal and Teamwork, Leadership, Operations, Recruitment and Selection, and General Administration.*

How Long Should Your Résumé be in Length?

Many of my clients ask me this question. My response to them is always shocking. We have been told over and over again that our résumé should only be one page long. Let's dispel this myth in hopes of freeing many of you from bondage. The truth is, if you are a person with extensive experience, then it is okay to have a two page résumé. Make sure you have some very important information on the second page that will inspire the interviewer to read it.

Your résumé should be one page if you are a recent graduate and don't have a lot of work experience. If you are this person, relax. Having a one page résumé can work to your advantage because it causes you to be mindful about the available space forces you to be clear and direct while highlighting your skills and accomplishments on your résumé.

It is very important that your résumé looks professional. Keep the following in mind when creating your résumé:

• Print your résumé on light colored stock paper (ex: white, beige, cream, off white, etc.).
• Include key words currently used in your industry or field.
• Proofread your résumé for errors.

- Identify key accomplishments.
- Ensure that employment dates are correct.
- Use powerful action verbs (ex: managed, created, analyzed, trained, implemented, etc.).
- Ensure that your résumé is quantifiable by including numbers, dollar signs, and percentages whenever possible.

Last but not least, please make sure that your résumé is legible and includes the following elements before you send it out to an employer:

- Your home contact information (name, address, zip code, home phone number, cell phone number, and E-mail address).
- Objective, stating the position of interest.
- Education, school(s) attended, or list of courses completed.
- Work experience statements using strong action verbs.
- Three major accomplishments from each position listed.
- Training received from places of employment.
- Community and volunteer involvement activities.
- Licenses and certifications received.
- Honors and awards received.
- Professional memberships.

If you would like to have your résumé evaluated prior to being sent out to potential employers, contact "Be Blessed" Career Consulting Inc. for a FREE Evaluation via E-mail: Beblessedcc@aol.com, Web site: www.BeBlessedCareerConsulting.com, or mail: P.O. Box 4373 Southfield, MI 48037. Be sure to have your cover letter and résumé proofread by a licensed human resource professional.

Personal Assignments

1. Find a quiet place and create a cover letter.

2. Find a quiet place and create a résumé.
3. Type both your résumé and cover letter in two Microsoft Word Documents.

4. Send your résumé and cover letter to "Be Blessed" Career Consulting Inc. to receive a FREE evaluation by a licensed human resource professional.

Prayer

Thank You Lord for giving me the spirit of excellence. Everything that I do in my job search is dedicated to You. My cover letter and résumé contain the necessary information that my future employer is looking for. I thank You in advance that my future employer will see Your character magnified in everything that I've done in my past places of employment and in the interviewing process. Thank You Lord for the spirit of excellence. Amen.

DECISIVENESS

CHAPTER ELEVEN

"A doubleminded man is unstable in all his ways."
- James 1:8

Decisiveness is defined as, *"The ability to recognize key factors and finalize difficult decisions"* (Character First, 2004). It involves getting immediately to the fundamental issues and making clear, concrete, absolute calls. 1 Corinthians 14:33 states, *"For God is not the author of confusion, but of peace.* When was the last time that you made a big decision in your life? What caused you to make the decision? How much research did you do first prior to making the decision? Did you seek the Lord for His guidance?

Studies have shown that people make better decisions after they have completed first a thorough research on the subject matter. Research is equally important in the job search process because it helps you to get the "big picture." It allows you to obtain additional information about the company and position to determine if there is a good fit. Would you agree that accepting a job is an important decision? If you answered no then you are sadly mistaken. Let me explain why.

According to *Workplace Wisdom Publishing's,* **"Using the Resources of God to Succeed at Work,"** people spend over 70 percent of their waking lives in work related activity. The decision to work for a company is extremely important, because you don't want to spend most of your life working in an environment that you do not enjoy. I would not want to spend seventy percent of my life being unhappy. Would you? Make the right decision by seeking God first. Get His direction for your life. Your life is worth it.

We will discuss two opportunities that you will get to demonstrate the character quality of decisiveness during your job search. First, we will review the importance of researching companies and job postings. Second, we will review the importance of job interviews.

Researching Company & Job Postings

There are many resources available for you to properly research potential employers. Most information can be obtained by accessing their company Web site. Popular search engines such as www.yahoo.com, www.altavista.com and www.google.com can locate the company Web site within seconds. My favorite Web site used to research companies for my clients is www.fortune.com.

For those of you that are not that knowledgeable about the Internet, I would recommend that you set aside some time and visit your local library to learn how to surf the web for yourself. Your public librarian can also provide you with other valuable resources to use to research companies for job postings.

It is very important that you take the time in the beginning of your job search to accurately review job postings before you complete an employment application or submit a cover letter and résumé to the employer. Key information to look for on a job posting is job title, qualification requirements, roles and responsibilities, travel requirements, normal working hours, position location (city, state), and hourly pay rate or beginning salary.

You may want to also compare the job posting to your résumé to see if it meets your personal career goals. Doing this step will also help you to prepare for the interview by identifying how your education and skills match the job requirements. This is important information that you should be prepared to share with the interviewer to help them make the connection that you are the correct person for the job because you meet all of the job requirements.

Preparing For a Job Interview

Have you ever heard the saying . . . "preparation is never lost time?" Well, this is true, especially when preparing for a job interview. Earlier in this chapter we talked about researching companies and job postings. Now we will spend time discussing the importance of preparing for job interviews.

Did you know that practicing your interviews will help improve your decision-making skills? You are probably asking, "How can you link practicing interviewing skills with decision making?" I submit to you that an interview is nothing more than a process where a person asks a series of questions to help them make a decision that you are the right person to hire for their company.

If a recruiter asks you a specific question about your previous work experience and feels that you did not listen closely enough to properly answer each question, believe me, it will be remembered and you will receive a lower rating on that portion of your interview.

It is important to do your best throughout the entire interviewing process. By mentally highlighting your valuable work experience and relevant skills, the recruiter will make the connection that you are the right person for the job.

Personal Assignments

1. Identify the last big decision that you made in your life. What caused you to make the decision? How much research did you complete? Did you seek the Lord for His guidance?

2. Identify 15 key things that you are looking for in your next employer. Rank them by order of importance. Why did you rank them in the order selected?

3. Identify key things that are needed in order for you to accept your next position. Seek God to ensure that your priorities are in the proper place.

Prayer

Thank You Lord for giving me the wisdom to make the right decisions in my job search. I will continue to seek Your face to ensure that I am in Your will always. Thank You for peace in advance as I research companies and interview with potential employers to determine my next career move. My personal goal is to ensure that I remain in the center of Your perfect will. I count this done. Amen.

PATIENCE

CHAPTER TWELVE

"But let patience have her perfect work, that ye may be
perfect and entire, wanting nothing."
James 1:4

P atience is defined as, *"the capacity to endure hardship, difficulty,*
or inconvenience without complaint. Patience emphasizes
calmness, self-control, and the willingness or ability to tolerate
delay" (The American Heritage® Dictionary English Language,
2000).

What are you in a hurry for? Do you actually think that you can
locate a job without God's help? Absolutely not! Sometimes the
things in life cause us to slow down, be patient, and wait on God.
Isn't this what we should be doing in the first place?

Don't get me wrong. You will need to take action on a daily basis
towards your job search, but just because you don't have a job now
doesn't mean that God isn't working on your behalf. So remember
to act like God, and to be patient as you go through your job search.

There may be days when you will get many job leads. There will be other days when it may appear that you didn't receive one. God is working things out for you. Just continue to believe and trust in Him as your Jehovah Jireh, (your Provider) and watch Him work things out for you.

During your season of patience wait on God and follow His lead. There will be a time in the near future when you will be working again. It's closer than you think. When that time arrives, don't forget to give God all of the glory, honor, and praise. We know that, *"Every good gift and every perfect gift is from above"* (James 1:17).

Wait on the Lord and be of good courage. Remember to let patience have her perfect work in you. Most books on searching for a job note that for every $10,000 annually that you desire to make in your next job, it will take you approximately 30 days to locate that position.   For example, if you desire to make $50,000 in your next job it would take approximately five months for you to locate appropriate employment.

"With God all things are possible" (Matthew 19:26). He doesn't need to operate within the world's standards. The real question is what do you believe? Are you willing to do your part to actively look for employment? As was discussed earlier, you will need to do your part before God can do His. You must exercise patience to remain in control. It is an important element in a successful job search.

So get out of your seat right now and begin to thank God for giving you patience during your job search. Ask Him to give you the wisdom to know where you should go, and what positions you should apply for. Give Him thanks for "Your New Job." Stand in faith that it will be revealed to you in due time. Learn to enjoy your season of patience. This too shall pass. There will be an opportunity for you to look back on this time in your life and remember how God gave you the resources, strength, and patience you needed during your job search.

Personal Assignments

1. Identify five areas that you need to demonstrate patience in your personal life.

2. Identify how you will demonstrate patience in your daily job search. What actions will you take to effectively demonstrate patience in the areas identified?

3. Identify three areas in your life when you didn't demonstrate patience. What happened?

4. List how you will demonstrate patience with recruiters, job headhunters, employment agencies, and company human resource professionals.

5. How will you demonstrate patience in the interviewing process?

Prayer

Lord, please give me the wisdom needed to know where I should go, and the positions that I need to apply for. Thank You for the new job that You have for me. Thank You for revealing to me my next position in due season. Thank You for giving me the resources, strength, wisdom, and patience during my job search. Amen.

HUMBLENESS

"If my people, which are called by name, shall humble themselves, and pray, and seek my face, and turn from their wicked ways; then I will hear from heaven, and will forgive their sin, and will heal their land."
-2 Chronicles 7:14

L ooking for a job can be quite humbling. It is especially difficult if you don't have the right character. Losing your job is not the end of the world. Making career changes is not the end of the world. Getting fired from your last job isn't the end of the world. Having an employment gap on your résumé isn't the end of the world. Are you getting the point yet? It is not the end of the world! These things can be overcome as long as your attitude is reflecting godly humility.

God hates pride. 1 Peter 5:5 states, *"For God resisteth the proud and giveth grace to the humble."* It is that simple. If you have a prideful heart during your job search, it will get in the way and stop the blessings that God has for you.

You need to be comfortable with asking people for help. God doesn't do anything in the earth unless we ask Him. Even if He has placed people in your path to bless you, nothing would come of it if you don't open your mouth, humble yourself and ask for help. Remember, God can use anything or anybody to bless you with your new job. You will need to do your part first. Be humble enough to accept help from others.

RESOURCES TO HELP YOU WITH YOUR JOB SEARCH

When you wake up in the morning, you should thank God for allowing you an opportunity to see another day, and for the resources that He has provided for you during your job search. Resources can come to you in many shapes and forms. I always tell my clients to keep their options open while looking for employment. You don't know where or how God will bless you with your next job. Don't put limits on God.

Below is a list of resources that you should consider using during your job search:

- ✦ Be Blessed Career Consulting Inc.
- ✦ Recruiters
- ✦ Job Head Hunters
- ✦ Job Fairs
- ✦ Temporary Employment Agencies
- ✦ Permanent Employment Agencies
- ✦ Contract Houses
- ✦ Sunday Newspaper Classified Section
- ✦ Company Web sites
- ✦ Job Search Web sites
- ✦ Employment Papers
- ✦ Employment Hotlines
- ✦ Family Members

- ✦ Friends
- ✦ Past Coworkers
- ✦ Past Competitors
- ✦ Past Vendors
- ✦ Past Suppliers
- ✦ Churches
- ✦ Unemployment Agencies
- ✦ Government Employment Offices
- ✦ City Offices
- ✦ State Offices
- ✦ Human Resource Departments
- ✦ Professional Clubs
- ✦ Professional Organizations
- ✦ Professional Associations
- ✦ Industry Trade Journals
- ✦ Industry Publications
- ✦ Industry Conventions
- ✦ Trade Shows
- ✦ Career Seminars and Workshops
- ✦ Trade Schools
- ✦ Public Libraries
- ✦ Vocational Schools
- ✦ Alumni Associations
- ✦ College or University Career Centers
- ✦ Professional Network Gatherings
- ✦ Social Events and Programs
- ✦ Job Shadowing Activities
- ✦ Summer Internships
- ✦ Mass Résumé Distribution
- ✦ E-mail Distribution List
- ✦ Radio Stations
- ✦ Television Stations
- ✦ Professional Sports Outings
- ✦ Local Community Buildings

- ✦ Speaking Engagements
- ✦ Company Open Houses
- ✦ Personnel Agencies
- ✦ Job Search Books and Resources
- ✦ Public Relations Directors
- ✦ Vice Presidents of organizations
- ✦ Union Houses
- ✦ Industry Newsletters

It is extremely important that you feel comfortable making the initial contact with the people and resources listed above. They may have or know of open positions in companies that you qualify for. You will have to be bold enough to swallow your pride and ask for assistance. Remember, the Lord can't do anything in the earth unless we ask Him. A person here on the earth won't know that you are looking for a job unless you ask them for help.

Personal Assignments

1. Identify 10 people that have asked to assist you with your job search, but you have not yet used their services. Contact them today and let them know how they can assist you.

2. Identify 20 people (not those already listed above) that you will contact to let them know that you will need their assistance in helping you locate employment. Call them this week to ask for assistance.

3. Identify contacts (ex: name, title, phone, E-mail, and fax number) for 30 of the resources listed in this chapter. Contact all resources this month to request assistance with your job search. Follow up with key resources monthly.

Prayer

Thank You Lord, for helping me to cast down pride in my life and replace it with humility. I trust in You for providing resources for me to use during my job search. I will feel comfortable in asking people for help. I know that receiving help from others is not a sign of weakness, but a sign of strength. I know that You are happy when we forget about our pride and allow people to bless us. Thanks for blessing me through people and resources. Amen.

MEEKNESS

CHAPTER FOURTEEN

"Blessed are the meek: for they shall inherit the earth."
- Matthew 5:5

A re you teachable, modest, and humble? In order to have a successful job search, you should be. Meekness is defined as, *"Showing patience and humility: gentle"* (Webster's II New Riverside Dictionary, 1996). God could be doing "A New Thing" in your life, and He wants to provide new resources for you. Will you let Him? Let God be God in your life. Let Him bring new ideas, people, resources and jobs into your life. The resources that the Lord uses are a blessing for you during your job search.

Years ago, finding a job could have been as easy as looking in the Sunday newspaper and sending your résumé to various companies. Nowadays, job seekers must use networking and access the Internet to send their résumés to companies (among many other resources) as a part of an effective job search strategy.

New job seekers must also contact employment agencies to take skill evaluation tests, attend job fairs, and visit company open houses. Stay open. Be flexible. Always be ready to learn something new. The world is changing, and so are the other candidates that are looking for employment. Use all of the skills that the Lord has equipped you with to stand out among the rest.

One way to remain teachable is to continue to take training classes while you are looking for a job. You can go to your local public library, employment career office, or a nearby training center such as New Horizons (www.newhorizons.com) and register for classes in the areas in which you need further development. There are knowledgeable people available to help you improve your skills. You can take classes to learn how to surf the Internet, send E-mails, or improve your business etiquette and computer skills. You will receive a certificate of completion for most classes attended that you can add to your résumé, or show during job interviews. The best benefit of all is that you can show God that you've demonstrated the character quality of meekness, and that you are "open and willing" to allow Him to teach you new things.

PERSONAL ASSIGNMENTS

1. Identify areas that you need to develop in (ex: computer software, grammar, business etiquette, project management, Internet usage, presentation skills, etc.).

2. Locate resources in your community where you can receive training (ex: unemployment office, library, employment agencies, or training centers).

3. Call the identified resources listed above to sign up for upcoming training sessions during your career transition.

4. Attend classes of interest. Keep copies of all certificates received. Add the titles and dates of your completed classes to your résumé.

Prayer

Thank you Lord for showing me new things. I am teachable. I am modest. I am humble. You know "all things." I just want to take this time to thank You for bringing resources my way to assist me with my job search. Amen.

LOVE

CHAPTER FIFTEEN

*"But I say unto you, love your enemies, bless them that
curse you, do good to them that hate you, and pray for them
which despitefully use you, and persecute you . . ."*
- Matthew 5:44

I realize that many of you may have been affected by corporate downsizing. I know how you must feel. I've been there before. The devil may have meant for it to defeat you. God will turn your situation around.

We often hear in the news media about company downsizing in order to save money. This may be your case, but it doesn't mean that you have been given the approval to hold a grudge against your previous employer.

Who is your source? Is it God or an employer? Hopefully by now you are realizing that God is your source, and that He will continue to provide for you as you go through a career transition.

In 1 Corinthians 13:4-8 (The Amplified Bible, 1987) it states,

"Love endures long and is patient and kind; love never is envious nor boils over with jealousy, is not boastful or vainglorious, does not display itself haughtily. It is not conceited (arrogant and inflated with pride); it is not rude (unmannerly) and does not act unbecomingly. Love (God's love in us) does not insist on its own rights or its own way, for it is not self-seeking; it is not touchy or fretful or resentful; it takes no account of the evil done to it (it pays no attention to a suffered wrong). It does not rejoice at injustice and unrighteousness, but rejoices when right and truth prevail. Love bears up under anything and everything that comes, is ever ready to believe the best of every person, its hopes are fadeless under all circumstances, and it endures everything (without weakening). Love never fails (never fades out or becomes obsolete or comes to an end)."

In Matthew 5:44 the Bible says that we are to love, bless, do good, and pray for our enemies. It may seem that your previous employer is your enemy. If you are holding hurt, pain and unforgiveness in your heart towards them then you are allowing the devil to win. Let the pain go. It's not worth it! The devil wants us to think that we have been abandoned by God. He wants you to hold on to unforgiveness. God's Word tells us that the Lord can bless you as you forgive others, and as you let go of the root of bitterness and unforgiveness. Let God's love rule in your heart towards your enemies. You will be able to do this when you truly believe that God is your source, not your past, present, or future employer!

Personal Assignments

1. What is your definition of love? How does it compare to 1 Corinthians 13:4-8?

2. Identify people that have hurt you in the past. List their names on a blank sheet of paper.

3. Go down your list and forgive everyone included. Say aloud, "Lord, I forgive (insert the person's name here) for (insert what he/she did to you). If you don't remember, forgive them anyway.

4. Think of a way that you can bless everyone listed above. If you experience difficulty with coming up with ideas, ask God to reveal to you what you should do.

5. Do everything that the Lord tells you to do. Write down the date and time when you've completed each assignment.

Prayer

Thank You Lord for the unconditional love that You've shown me. Because of You, I now know that I can love and forgive others. Even though my job may have been lost due to corporate downsizing, I know that you will turn this situation around and make it good for me. At this moment, I forgive all of the people that have trespassed against me in the past. I no longer hold on to hurt or pain. I only hold unto Your love in me. Lord, bless them with the desires of their heart as it conforms with Your will. Amen.

FAITH

CHAPTER SIXTEEN

"For we walk by faith, not by sight."
- 2 Corinthians 5:7

The next characteristic that you should have for a successful job search is faith. Faith is defined as, *"Belief that is not based on proof"* (Random House Unabridged Dictionary, 1997). Now, what is the substance that you are hoping for? Notice that I started the sentence off with the word "now." What kind of job or career do you want at this very moment? Have you really thought about it? How would you like for God to move on your behalf in your current job search? You must first know what you want before you can ask God for it. Let's take a moment to find out what the Word says about faith . . .

"And when he saw their faith, he said unto him, Man, thy sins are forgiven thee." *- Luke 5:20*

". . . But the just shall live by his faith." *- Habakkuk 2:4*

"Jesus answered and said unto them, Verily I say unto you,
if ye have faith, and doubt not, ye shall not only do this which is
done to the fig tree, but also if ye shall say unto this mountain, be
thou removed, and be thou cast into the sea; it shall be done.
- Matthew 21:21

"For I say, through the grace given unto me, to every man that is
among you, not to think of himself more highly than he ought to think;
but to think soberly, according as God hath dealt to every man the
measure of faith." - Romans 12:3

"Above all, taking the shield of faith, where with ye shall be able to
quench all the fiery darts of the wicked." - Ephesians 6:16

"But without faith it is impossible to please him; for he that cometh
to God must believe that he is, and that he is a rewarder of them that
diligently seek him." - Hebrews 11:6

"Even so faith, if it hath not works, is dead, being alone." - James 2:17

"So then faith cometh by hearing, and hearing by the word of God."
- Romans 10:17

"Now faith is the substance of things hoped for, the evidence
of things not seen." - Hebrews 11:1

What are you hoping for? Do you want to work for a large company or steward a business for the kingdom of God? Do you prefer to work in a plant environment or in a corporate office setting? Do you want to look for a new job in your same field or do you want to make a career change? Whatever your desire is, take the time before God in prayer regarding your personal career and purpose in life. Through prayer, reading the Word and research, the Lord will reveal to you your purpose in life. He will make "substance" the very thing that you have been standing in faith for. Have an open mind and heart. Allow the Holy Spirit to reveal to you your purpose. He will show you things to come.

PERSONAL ASSIGNMENTS

1. Make a list of the things that you are believing God for.

2. Praise God every day for the next three months for providing you with the things on your list, even if it's unseen.

3. Thank God for supplying your needs today.

Prayer

I thank You Lord for providing me with the desires of my heart. I believe in Your Word. 2 Corinthians 5:7 says we walk by faith and not by sight. I thank You for my job, even if I can't see it right now. I know that You will make a way for me and I want to thank You for it now. Amen.

WISDOM

CHAPTER SEVENTEEN

"In the lips of him that hath understanding wisdom is found."
- Proverbs 10:13

Wₑ all need wisdom in order to have a successful job search. I can't think of a better place to study wisdom than in the Word of God. Let us find out what the Bible says about getting wisdom.

"How much better is it to get wisdom than gold! and to get understanding rather to be chosen than silver!" - Proverbs 16:16

"And wisdom and knowledge shall be the stability of thy times."
- Isaiah 33:6

"The fear of the Lord is the beginning of wisdom . . ." - Proverbs 9:10

"If any of you lack wisdom, let him ask God, that giveth to all men liberally . . ." - James 1:5

In this chapter, the scripture that we will focus on is James 3:17, *"But the wisdom that is from above is first pure, then peaceable, gentle, and easy to be entreated, full of mercy and good fruits."* Our focus will be on these six words — they are:

- Pure
- Peaceable
- Gentle
- Easy
- Mercy
- Good Fruits

The Lord revealed to me how James 3:17 can easily be applied to a person currently going through a career transition. Lets begin with the word pure. . .

PURE

While preparing for an interview it is important to complete company research. This will allow you to identify pure, innocent, genuine, straight to the point, simple, good and honest questions that could be asked by the interviewer. This is a key step in the interview process since the purpose of the job interview is to gather information about the company and the position to determine if there is a good fit for you and, most importantly, to determine if this is where God wants you to be! You must first stop to pray to God for wisdom, and then gather knowledge about the company and any open positions of interest.

One way to gather knowledge about the position is to ask questions. I can remember many times asking candidates if they had questions for me about the company or position during an interview. Most of the time they said, "No I don't."

Every time this occurred it appeared to me as if they were not interested in the position. It showed me that they did not properly prepare for the interview. That doesn't look good in your interview file. So speak up and ask the recruiter questions at the end of an interview. You can let the interviewer know that you've done your research, and that you are very interested in the position by simply asking questions about the position.

To assist you in feeling comfortable in asking questions during the interview, I have enclosed a list of key questions that you may want to ask during an interview:

✦ Who will the person in this position be reporting to?
✦ Where is the position located?
✦ What qualities do you look for in an applicant for this position?
✦ Why did this position become available?
✦ What are the normal working hours for a person in this position?
✦ What is the natural career path for a person in this position?
✦ How often are performance reviews conducted?
✦ How will the performance of the person in this position be evaluated?
✦ Are performance reviews tied to compensation or are they handled separately?
✦ How much travel is required for this position?
✦ How many people will be reporting to the person in this position?
✦ What would an average day on the job entail?
✦ What would the most important responsibility in this job be?
✦ What additional responsibilities would I have in this position?
✦ Will the person that is hired for this position receive formalized training? Or will he/she receive on-the-job training? How long is the training program?
✦ How many candidates have you interviewed for this position?

- ✦ How many candidates do you have left to interview?
- ✦ How long has this position been open?
- ✦ What equipment and computer software is required for this position?
- ✦ What type of person are you looking for?
- ✦ What are the goals of the department for the next five years?
- ✦ What are the goals of the company for the next five years?
- ✦ What function will I play in these goals?
- ✦ Who are other key people that the person in this position will work with?
- ✦ What particular areas of this job have people had difficulty with in the past?
- ✦ What is the last person hired for this job doing now?
- ✦ What future changes do you see for this company?
- ✦ Do you plan on reducing head count (workforce) in your company or department anytime soon? If so, how many? How soon?
- ✦ Will the person hired for this position be working in a team environment or independently?
- ✦ What do you see as the biggest areas that need improvement in your company?
- ✦ What steps are in place to ensure that your managers value diversity and personal worklife balance in your organization?
- ✦ What program does your company offer that supports employee family flexibility hours and worklife integration?
- ✦ Tell me more about your company's employee mentoring program.
- ✦ What significant changes has your company experienced over the past two years?
- ✦ What has been your career path?
- ✦ What are the next steps in the interviewing process? When should I expect to hear from you?
- ✦ Do you have any reservations about hiring me for the position? If so what are they?

✦ What are good qualities that I possess that make me an excellent candidate for the job?

The interviewer normally allocates time at the end of the interview for you to ask questions. Remember to use this time wisely. Think of four to eight questions to ask during the interview. You will impress the interviewer, but most importantly, you will gain valuable knowledge about the company that will assist you in making the right decision about your career.

PEACEABLE

Peace is defined as, *"freedom from disquieting feelings and thoughts: serenity"* (Webster's II New Riverside Dictionary, 1996). After seeking God about your career, researching the company and asking questions during the interview, look to God to give you peace about the position. We know that God is not the author of confusion, but of peace . . . (1 Corinthians 14:33). Check your "gut" feeling to see if you have peace about taking the job.

GENTLE

Gentleness is defined as, *"to be easily handled or managed"* (Webster's II New Riverside Dictionary, 1996). The Holy Spirit will minister to you and give you a gentle nudge in your spirit if the position is the one for you. God will not force you to make a decision. He is a gentleman. He will allow you an opportunity to make up your own mind.

EASY

The word "easy" is defined as, *"being not hard or difficult; requiring no great labor or effort"* (Random House Unabridged Dictionary, 1997). Many people may think that deciding to accept a position is difficult, but it is not. Actually, accepting a job offer is a very easy thing to do if you have spent time with God in prayer, researched the company thoroughly, and have received peace to move forward with the new opportunity.

I believe that we sometimes make things more difficult than they should be. If we consult with God first in everything that we do (including our job decisions) we can receive "inside information" from the Holy Spirit as to what to do, then we can have peace in the process.

During the interview process you should have been seeking God about His direction regarding the position. You should have been asking for wisdom and knowledge about the position to make a decision that is pleasing to God. If you haven't gone to God about your next career move, it is not too late. You can go to Him right now. Ask that He reveal to you the purpose for your life, and for the career that He has created for you.

MERCY

Mercy is defined as, *"Something that gives evidence of divine favor"* (Random House Unabridged Dictionary, 1997). Now, after you have gone to God about your career and purpose in life, completed your research on respective employers, asked the interviewer pure, genuine, and honest questions, received peace and a gentle nudge from the Holy Spirit about the position, and made your easy decision to accept the position, you will receive mercy from God to learn the job, and to do it successfully.

Starting a new job can be both exciting and nerve-racking all at the same time. Everyone wants to do a great job and learn fast in their new position. We may make some mistakes along the way, but that is where God's mercy comes in. There have been times in our lives where we have "missed it," but by the grace and mercy of God we are kept in the game.

When was the last time that you missed the mark and God saved you and gave you another chance to do it right? This is exactly what God will do for you in your new position if you are where He wants you to be. He will place people around you to help you obtain the knowledge and wisdom to complete the job successfully. Even though you may not have an identified "Trainer or Mentor" to help you in your new position remember that all wisdom and knowledge comes from God. All that you need to do is tap into His power. Ask the Holy Spirit to come upon you for power to do your new job successfully. Watch the Lord operate in your life with the mercy of God.

GOOD FRUITS

When you are operating in God's perfect will, you can't help but to produce "Good Fruits." The job that you have will become second nature to you. There will be ease in doing it. Your supervisor may give you more responsibilities because you have excelled in completing the task at hand. Your co-workers will be thankful that you are on their team because you bring value to it. Your customers will give you "raving reviews" to your boss because you exhibited great customer service. Your boss will see your good fruits and will give you high marks on your performance review because you have shown yourself faithful and worthy. God will promote you in due season. Promotion comes from the Lord.

PERSONAL ASSIGNMENTS

1. Spend time in prayer this week asking God for wisdom in your job search.

2. Make a list of what God reveals to you in prayer. Complete every task that He gives to you.

3. Review the list of questions that you can ask in an interview as listed above.

4. Identify 4-8 questions that you may want to ask a potential employer in upcoming interviews.

Prayer

Thank You Lord for wisdom and understanding. Even though my natural mind may not understand why I am in the present situation in my life, I do know that my steps are ordered by You. Continue to minister to me about the next steps that I should take in my job search. Thank You for providing me with "inside information." I will do what You instruct me to do. Amen.

PART C

A Closer Look at Your Commitment

SALARY NEGOTIATIONS: YOU HAVE NOT, BECAUSE YOU ASK NOT!

". . . ye have not, because ye ask not." - James 4:2

Wow! Sometimes things are just that simple. As I've stated earlier, sometimes we make things more difficult than they have to be. The sad story is many of us do this when it comes to salary negotiating.

Reflect for a moment about how you negotiated your starting salary with your current or previous employer. Did you research your industry first to determine your salary pay range? What resources did you use to locate this salary information? Did you initiate salary discussions or did your employer? Did you take some time to consider the offer before you accepted the job? Did you ask for more personal time off or more vacation time? Did you ask to modify your company benefits? Did you ask for a higher starting salary than what was originally offered? Did you ask for an earlier performance review that is tied to your direct compensation? Did you really negotiate your salary?

If you answered "No" to any of the questions above, then I regret to inform you that you did not properly negotiate your starting salary and may have missed an opportunity to make more money. There is still hope.

SALARY RESEARCH

Throughout my 13 years working in human resources, I have found that a lot of people don't feel comfortable in talking about money in the interviewing process. The main reason for this is because they don't know where to go to properly research salary information. Some of the resources that I use to research starting salaries are:

- ✦ Company job postings.
- ✦ Newspaper classified advertisements.
- ✦ Company human resource professionals.
- ✦ Compensation surveys.
- ✦ Job search Internet Web sites.
- ✦ Occupational outlook handbook.
- ✦ Recruiters.
- ✦ Job headhunters.
- ✦ Temporary and permanent employment agencies.
- ✦ Professional organizations and associations.

The Internet can be a wonderful source to use to conduct research on starting salaries. The following are a few of my favorite Web sites:

www.jobstar.org
www.careerbuilder.com
www.csp.msu.edu/cdc/career
www.monstertrak.com
www.wetfeet.com

www.shrm.org
www.hotjobs.com
www.wageweb.com
www.bestjobsusa.com
www.abbott-langer.com
http://stats.bls.gov

Once you have completed your thorough research you will be more comfortable. You will know how much money you should ask for in the job interview. Lets talk about when to begin the salary negotiating process.

SALARY NEGOTIATING

When is the best time to discuss money with a potential employer? Please select one of the following answers:

A) Before the phone interview.
B) During the phone interview.
C) During the face-to-face interview.
D) Once you have received an actual job offer from the potential employer.

Before I give you the answer to the question, let's review why it is important to feel comfortable talking about starting salaries with a potential employer:

> ✦ You may get a higher salary and benefits package if you don't take the first offer made.
> ✦ You may get more vacation time, better health coverage, and tuition reimbursement.
> ✦ You will be happier in your new job.
> ✦ You will be happier with your new employer.

✦ You will have a stronger desire to stay with the company longer.
✦ You may get a higher starting salary.
✦ You may get a higher starting salary.
✦ You may get a higher starting salary.

Do you get the picture yet? You may get a higher starting salary! Remember all of your bonuses will be based on the starting base rate. In Proverbs 10:22 it states, *"The blessing of the Lord, it maketh rich, and he addeth no sorrow with it."* Acknowledge God in your salary negotiating stage and get ready to "Be Blessed!"

Let's get back to the question at hand. When is the best time to talk about salary with a potential employer during the job search process? The answer is . . .

> **D) Once you have received an actual job offer from the potential employer.**

During all of the other stages in the interviewing process the employer is in their "Budgeting Stage." When the employer is in this stage they are basically concerned with their budget and not concerned with what you have to bring to their organization. At this point they really don't know if you are qualified for the job. That is why they have decided to interview you in the first place.

If you attempt to begin discussing your starting salary with an employer prior to the extension of a job offer, chances are you will turn the interviewer off because you will appear to be more interested in the money than the position.

THE RESPONSE

If by chance an employer should be bold enough to ask you about your salary requirements before offering you the job you may want to say something like this . . .

"I am flexible about my starting salary and we can talk about that at a later time; however, at this time I am more interested in learning about your open position to ensure that I am the right candidate for the job. Can you tell me more information about the responsibilities of a person in this position?"

A response like this will shock the interviewer, and will put them at ease regarding the money. In your statement you discussed that you will talk about the money later, but that you are more interested in the position. The main goal for the interviewer is to make sure that they find the right person for the job. Your statement eases their mind, because the interviewer will quickly realize that the both of you have a major common goal . . . "Finding a Perfect Fit for Yourself and the Company."

Let's take a moment to cover a few salary negotiating do's and dont's:

+ Don't talk about money before the job offer is made.
+ Don't be the first person to talk about money.
+ Don't talk about money during the phone interview.
+ Don't talk about money at the first interview.
+ Don't commit yourself to a specific number (think ranges).
+ Don't tell the interviewer the minimum starting salary you will accept.
+ Do express interest and excitement about the job.
+ Be confident - You've done your research and know what you are worth!

+ Do have a salary range in mind before negotiations begin.
+ Do make sure that you've conducted your salary research before the interview.
+ Do tell the interviewer the mid to high pay range that you will consider discussing after the job has been offered to you.
+ Do be sure to consider other non compensatory benefits (ie: tuition reimbursement, vacation, holidays, personal days, company car, telecommuting, health club memberships, relocation, cost of living adjustments, child day care, mentoring, training, travel perks, profit sharing, and signing bonuses).
+ Do keep all salary discussion friendly and upbeat.
+ Do get your job offer in writing.
+ Thank God for your new job and pay increase.
+ Celebrate. Your hard work has paid off!

We know that *the love of money is the root of all evil* (1 Timothy 6:10). Having a lot of money isn't wrong, but the love of it is. Do you love money so much that it is more important to you than being in the job or career that God has ordained for you? I hope that the answer to that question was "no" and that you will spend time with God to ask Him to reveal your career path to you. God loves you so much that He wants to see you highly favored and empowered to prosper in your finances. *He will supply all of your needs according to His riches in glory by Christ Jesus* (Philippians 4:19). Trust Him.

Personal Assignments

1. Visit each Web site listed in this chapter and gather information from your field of interest. What areas are you interested in? What are the educational requirements? Is there a degree, license, or certification requirement for the position you are interested in? How many years of experience do you have? What is the average starting salary for a person in the selected job?

2. Identify 2-3 professional organizations or associations in your field of interest. Visit their websites to see the current job postings. What are the starting salaries for the positions posted?

3. Identify the pay range that you would accept from your next employer. Be prepared to explain how you came up with the range.

4. Practice the salary negotiation statement listed in this chapter so you can effectively respond to employer inquiries about your preferred starting salary before a position is offered to you.

Prayer

Thank you Lord for my increase. I trust in You to provide for all of my needs. Your Word says, "Wisdom is a defence, and money is a defence: but the excellency of knowledge is, that wisdom giveth life to them that have it." (Ecclesiastes 7:12). Thank You for giving me life and knowledge as to how to research and negotiate starting salaries. "To God be the Glory." Amen.

PERSONAL JOB SEARCH COMMITMENT PAGE

I _____ will do what
is needed to have a successful job search. I will get up early and
complete all of my daily assignments. I realize that looking for
a job is a job. I will be diligent as I commit to this process. I will
dedicate my job search to the Lord, and demonstrate His character
throughout the entire job search process. I will be diligent,
resourceful, bold, humble and decisive. I will show self-control,
strive for excellence and use wisdom. I will demonstrate love,
patience, faith, and humility during my career transition.

_____

Signature

_____   _____

Date   Time

PART D

A Closer Look at the Blessings

WORDS TO STAND ON DURING YOUR JOB SEARCH

"For with the heart man believeth unto righteousness and
with the mouth confession is made unto salvation."
- Romans 10:10

It is important to have a positive confession during your job search. Many times people look at their current circumstance with despair. It is important to remember "Who you are in Christ," even while looking for employment. I invite you to take a moment to read the following scriptures aloud. My prayer is that they will uplift your spirit and encourage you as you go through your job search.

I AM...

Speaking boldly as I ought to speak (Ephesians 6:18)

Walking not after the flesh but after the Spirit (Romans 8:1)

Free from the law of sin and death (Romans 8:2)

Rejoicing with Joy unspeakable and Full of Glory (1 Peter 1:8)

Abiding in Him (1 John 2:27)

Abiding with God in my calling (1 Corinthians 7:24)

Keeping His commandments (1 John 3:24)

Free...indeed (John 8:36)

Forgetting those things which are behind (Philippians 3:14)

Reaching forth unto those things which are before (Philippians 3:14)

Redeemed from the Hand of the Enemy (Psalms 107:2)

Saved by Grace Through Faith (Ephesians 2:8)

Redeemed from the Curse of the Law (Galatians 3:13)

Delivered from the Powers of Darkness (Colossians 1:13)

Led by the Spirit of God (Romans 8:14)

Kept in Safety Wherever I Go (Psalm 91:11)

Casting All My Care on Jesus (1 Peter 5:7)

Strong in the Lord and in the Power of His Might (Ephesians 6:10)

Doing All Things through Christ Who Strengthens Me (Philippians 4:13)

An Heir of God and a Joint Heir with Jesus (Romans 8:17)

Observing and Doing the Lord's Commandments (Deuteronomy 28:6)

Blessed Coming in and Blessed Going out (Deuteronomy 28:12)

Blessed with all Spiritual Blessings (Ephesians 1:3)

Healed by His Stripes (1 Peter 2:24)

Exercising My Authority over the Enemy (Luke 10:19)

Above Only and Not Beneath (Deuteronomy 28:13)

More than a Conqueror (Romans 8:37)

Not Moved by What I See (2 Corinthians 4:18)

Walking by Faith and Not by Sight (2 Corinthians 5:7)

Bringing Every Thought into Captivity (2 Corinthians 10:5)

The Righteousness of God in Christ (2 Corinthians 5:21)

The Light of the World (Matthew 5:14)

Continually Praising the Lord with My Mouth (Psalm 34:1)

Loving the Lord My God with All of my Heart (Luke 10:27)

Loving my Neighbor as Myself (Luke 10:27)

Doer of God's Word and not a Hearer Only (James 1:22)

Not Conformed to this World (Romans 12:2)

Transformed by the Renewing of my Mind (Romans 12:2)

Proving what that Good, and Acceptable and Perfect Will of God is (Romans 12:2)

Strong in the Faith that is in Christ Jesus (1 Timothy. 2:1)

Wise unto Salvation through Faith which is in Christ (2 Timothy 3:15)

Bold (Ephesians 3:12)

Holding fast to the form of Sound Words (1 Timothy 1:13)

Anointed to Preach the Gospel to the poor (Luke 4:18)

Anointed to Heal the Broken Hearted (Luke 4:18)

Not Entangled with the affairs of this life (2 Timothy 2:4)

Living in Faith for the Just shall Live by Faith (Romans 1:17)

Shewing my Faith by my Works (James 2:18)

Not afraid, I Only Believe (Mark 5:36)

Serving the Lord My God (Joshua 24:24)

Obeying His Voice (Joshua 24:24)

At Thy Word I Will (Luke 5:5)

A Fragrance of the Knowledge of God in this World
(2 Corinthians 2:14)

Made All things to All Men that I Might, By All Means, Save Some
(1 Corinthians 9:22)

Temperate in All Things (1 Corinthians 9:25)

Keeping under My Body and bringing it into Subjection
(1 Corinthians 9:27)

Kind one to another, tenderhearted, forgiving another
(Ephesians 4:32)

Perfect even as my Father which is in Heaven is Perfect
(Matthew 5:48)

Not doubtful of mind (Luke 12:29)

Not conformed to this world (Romans 12:2)

Transformed by the renewing of my mind (Romans 12:2)

Proving what is that good, and acceptable, and perfect will of God
(Romans 12:2)

Holy in all manner of conversation (1 Peter 1:15)

Believing those things which I say shall come to pass (Mark 11:23)

Calling those things that be not as though they were until they are
(Romans 4:17)

Forgiving others as I pray (Mark 11:24)

Freely justified by His grace through redemption in Christ Jesus (Romans 3:24)

Blessed with all spiritual blessings in Heavenly places in Christ (Ephesians 1:3)

Fearfully and wonderfully made (Psalm 139:14)

PERSONAL ASSIGNMENTS

1. Meditate on the I AM Scriptures.

2. Go to a quiet place and record all of the I AM scriptures on a tape recorder.

3. Listen to the tape every morning before you begin your job search to get the scriptures into your spirit.

4. When obstacles come your way, "Speak Out" the scriptures that come to mind and watch God move in that situation.

Prayer

I thank You Lord for reminding me who I am. I am so grateful for Your Word and Your love. Thank You for providing direction and comfort for me. You are my everything, and I just want to thank You for Your presence and for being in my life. Your Word is true. I will stand on Your Word every day of my life. Amen.

APPENDIX B
BLESSED IS . . .

"Blessed are they that hear the word of God, and keep it."
- Luke 11:28

Before we can claim that we want to be highly favored and empowered to prosper in our job search, we must first understand what it means to "Be Blessed." I have included a list of examples of what it means to "Be Blessed" by the Word of God. So sit back and experience God's blessings.

"Blessed is the man that maketh the LORD his trust, and respecteth not the proud, nor such as turn aside to lies." - Psalm 40:4

"Blessed is he that considereth the poor: the LORD will deliver him in time of trouble." - Psalm 41:1

"Blessed is the man whom thou choosest, and causest to approach unto thee, that he may dwell in thy courts: we shall be satisfied with the goodness of thy house, even of thy holy temple." - Psalm 65:4

*"Blessed are they that dwell in thy house: they will
be still praising thee. Selah." - Psalm 84:4*

*"Blessed is the man whose strength is in thee; in whose
heart are the ways of them." - Psalm 84:5*

*"Blessed is the people that know the joyful sound: they shall walk,
O Lord, in the light of thy countenance." - Psalm 89:15*

*"Blessed are they that keep judgement, and he that doeth
righteousness at all times." - Psalm 106:3*

*"Blessed is the man that feareth the LORD, that delighteth
greatly in his commandments." - Psalm 112:1*

*"Blessed are the undefiled in the way, who walk
in the law of the LORD." - Psalm 119:1*

*"Blessed are they that keep his testimonies, and that seek
him with the whole heart." - Psalm 119:2*

*"Blessed is everyone that feareth the LORD;
that walketh in his ways." - Psalm 128:1*

"Blessed are they that keep my ways." - Proverbs 8:32

*"Blessed is the man that heareth me, watching daily at
my gates, waiting at the posts of my doors." - Proverbs 8:34*

*"Blessed is the man that trusteth in the LORD,
and whose hope the Lord is." - Jeremiah 17:7*

*"Blessed are the poor in spirit: for theirs is the kingdom of heaven."
- Matthew 5:3*

*"Blessed are they that mourn: for they shall be comforted."
- Matthew 5:4*

*"Blessed are the meek: for they shall inherit the earth."
- Matthew 5:5*

"Blessed are they which do hunger and thirst after righteousness: for they shall be filled." - Matthew 5:6

"Blessed are the merciful: for they shall obtain mercy." – Matthew 5:7

"Blessed are the pure in heart: for they shall see God." – Matthew 5:8

"Blessed are the peacemakers: for they shall be called the children of God." - Matthew 5:9

"Blessed are they which are persecuted for righteousness' sake: for theirs is the kingdom of heaven." – Matthew 5:10

"Blessed are ye, when men shall revile you, and persecute you, and shall say all manner of evil against you falsely, for my sake." - Matthew 5:11

"But blessed are your eyes, for they see: and your ears, for they hear." - Matthew 13:16

" . . . Blessed is he that cometh in the name of the Lord." – Matthew 23:39

". . . Blessed is the fruit of thy womb." – Luke 1:42

"Blessed is she that believed: for there shall be a performance of those things which were told her from the Lord." – Luke 1:45

". . . Blessed be ye poor: for yours is the kingdom of God." – Luke 6:20

"Blessed are ye that hunger now: for ye shall be filled. Blessed are ye that weep now: for ye shall laugh." – Luke 6:21

"Blessed are ye, when men shall hate you, and when they shall separate you from their company, and shall reproach you, and cast out your name as evil, for the Son of man's sake." – Luke 6:22

"Blessed is he, whosoever shall not be offended in me." – Luke 7:23

*"Blessed are the eyes which see the things
that ye see." – Luke 10:23*

*"Blessed are those servants, whom the lord when
he cometh shall find watching . . ." – Luke 12:37*

*"Blessed is he that shall eat bread in the kingdom of God."
– Luke 14:15*

*"Blessed are the barren, and the wombs that never bare . . ."
– Luke 23:29*

*"Blessed are they whose iniquities are forgiven,
and whose sins are covered." - Romans 4:7*

*"Blessed is the man that endureth temptation: for
when he is tried, he shall receive the crown of life, which
the Lord hath promised to them that love him." - James 1:12*

*"Blessed is he that readeth, and they that hear the words
of this prophecy, and keep those things which are written
therein: for the time is at hand." - Revelation 1:3*

*"Blessed are they which are called unto the marriage
supper of the Lamb . . ." - Revelation 19:9*

Personal Assignments

1. Read scriptures listed in this chapter.

2. Meditate on the scriptures to get them into your spirit.

3. Identify 10 key scriptures to stand on during your job search.

Prayer

Lord, I thank You for sharing with me what it means to "Be Blessed" in Your Word. I will meditate on Your Word during my job search. Thank You for sending favor ahead of me as I network with others and interview with potential employers. I am highly favored, and I am empowered to prosper. I just want to thank You in advance for all of the blessings that You have in store for me. Amen.

APPENDIX C

HOW TO BE BLESSED
IN YOUR DAILY LIFE

*"That if thou shalt confess with thy mouth the Lord Jesus, and
shalt believe in thine heart that God hath raised him from
the dead, thou shalt be saved."*
- Romans 10:9

As you have read, all blessings come from the Lord. In order to truly "Be Blessed" in your personal life, you need Jesus Christ. Jesus Christ came to the world to redeem the world. He loved you so much that He died for you. He took our sins to the cross so that we could have eternal life with Him. Wasn't that an awesome thing to do for us? That shows us how much God loves us. If you have not already done so, will you give your life to Him today? He is waiting to bless you. Please take a moment to read this prayer aloud.

Prayer

Thank You Lord for saving my life. Lord, thank You for being with me every step throughout my job search. I believe that You died for me on the cross at Calvary. I also believe that You carried my sins for me. I believe that they put You in a grave, but You are alive "Right Now." Dear Lord, come into my life right now! Save me now! Forgive me for the times that I've missed the mark. I accept You as my personal Lord and Savior. I am whole. I am new. I am BLESSED (Highly Favored and Empowered to Prosper), In Jesus name. Amen.

APPENDIX D

A PRAYER OF BLESSINGS
OVER YOUR LIFE
(FROM ME TO YOU)

I would like to encourage you to do what's needed to have a successful job search. My prayer for you is that you remember to get up early to spend time with the Lord. Complete all of your daily assignments. Realize that looking for a job "Is a Job," and to be diligent as you commit to the process. Above all, dedicate your life (including your job search) to the Lord. Demonstrate His character throughout the entire job search process. Be diligent, resourceful, bold and decisive. Show self-control, strive for excellence and use wisdom. Demonstrate love, patience, faith and humility during your career transition.

Don't forget Deuteronomy 28:1-14 which reads,

"And it shall come to pass, if thou shalt hearken diligently unto the voice of the Lord thy God, to observe and to do all his commandments which I command thee this day, that the Lord thy God will set thee on high above

all nations of the earth: these blessings shall come on thee, and overtake thee, if thou shalt hearken unto the voice of the Lord thy God. Blessed shalt thou be in the city, and blessed shalt thou be in the field. Blessed shall be the fruit of thy body, and the fruit of thy ground, and the fruit of thy cattle, the increase of thy kine, and the flocks of thy sheep. Blessed shall be thy basket and thy store.

"Blessed shalt thou be when thou comest in, and blessed shalt thou be when thou goest out. The Lord shall cause thine enemies that rise up against thee to be smitten before thy face: they shall come out against thee one way, and flee before thee seven ways. The Lord shall command the blessing upon thee in thy storehouses, and in all that thou settest thine hand unto; and he shall bless thee in the land which the Lord thy God giveth thee. The Lord shall establish thee an holy people unto himself, as he hath sworn unto thee, if thou shalt keep the commandments of the Lord thy God, and walk in his ways.

"And all people of the earth shall see that thou art called by the name of the LORD; and they shall be afraid of thee. And the Lord shall make thee plenteous in goods, in the fruit of thy body, and in the fruit of thy cattle, and in the fruit of thy ground, in the land which the LORD sware unto thy fathers to give thee. The Lord shall open unto thee his good treasure, the heaven to give the rain unto thy land in his season, and to bless all the work of thine hand: and thou shalt lend unto many nations, and thou shalt not borrow. And the LORD shall make thee the head, and not the tail; and thou shalt be above only, and thou shalt not be beneath; if that thou hearken unto the commandments of the LORD thy God, which I command thee this day, to observe and to do them: And thou shalt not go aside from any of the words which I command thee this day, to the right hand, or to the left, to go after other gods to serve them."

PART E

A Closer Look at "Be Blessed" Career Consulting Inc.

. . . for the people had a mind to work!

ABOUT THE AUTHOR

Kimberly Anne Benjamin started *"Be Blessed" Career Consulting Inc.* in 2002 to be a resource for people who are in need of assistance in career planning, new business development and personal goal setting. Ms. Benjamin teaches invaluable skills and insights that assist organizations and individuals in building workable alliances by demonstrating godly character qualities.

Skilled in administration and action planning Ms. Benjamin incorporates experiential learning techniques in her work. In her seminars, Ms. Benjamin addresses the effects of changes in ones' career. Her approach facilitates dialogue and understanding between seminar participants. Ms. Benjamin also specializes in helping employees to identify the career that is best for them, and in providing resources needed for a successful transition.

Ms. Benjamin has over 13 years of experience in the human resources area. She works to oversee development of such areas as Diversity and Worklife Integration, Succession Planning, Training,

Recruitment and Selection, and New Hire Orientations. Ms. Benjamin has worked as a human resource professional at major companies, such as Ford Motor Company, General Motors, ITT Industries, Wal-mart, Toys-R-Us, and Kelsey Hayes.

Born and raised in Lansing, Michigan, Ms. Benjamin brings a unique perspective and a personal passion to her seminars. Ms. Benjamin received her Bachelor of Science Degree in Merchandise Management and Marketing from Eastern Michigan University in 1992 and a Master of Arts Degree in Labor Relations and Human Resource Management from Wayne State University in 1997. Ms. Benjamin is a certified Professional in Human Resources (PHR) through the Human Resource Certification Institute. Ms. Benjamin is also a member of the Society of Human Resource Management (SHRM) and a member of the Human Resources Association of Greater Detroit (HRAGD).

Ms. Benjamin has made it her mission to help people have a successful career transition. She uses simple language, action planning principles, and shares her personal stories and experiences as a human resource professional with her clients throughout all of her seminars. Her uniqueness comes from the time she takes to understand the pressures and challenges of her clients as she customizes a program action plan to meet their specific needs.

To contact Kimberly Anne Benjamin or to request information on her availability to speak, facilitate, coach, or for a consultation, write to:

"Be Blessed" Career Consulting Inc.
P.O. Box 4373, Southfield, MI 48037
or call **(586) 718-2571** *or send an*
E-mail to **Beblessedcc@aol.com**
or visit the website at
www.BeBlessedCareerConsulting.com

ABOUT "BE BLESSED" CAREER CONSULTING INC.

Our Primary Mission
To be a resource to people who are in need of assistance in career planning, new business development and personal goal setting.

Our Goal
To let people know that they can be highly favored and empowered to prosper in their job search while providing them with valuable resources to ensure that they have what is needed to experience a successful career transition.

Product & Service Offerings
Two Hour Personal Consultation

Cover Letter and Résumé Evaluation

Cover Letter and Résumé Creation

Thank You Letter Creation

Personal Job Interview Analysis

200 + Recruiter and Headhunter Book and Labels

My Personalized 30 Day Job Search Plan Work Book

How to Be Highly Favored and Empowered to Prosper In Your Job Search Book

How to Be Highly Favored and Empowered to Prosper In Your Job Search Work Book

Seminars & Workshops

What To Do If You Get Laid Off or Let Go

Finding a Perfect Career

Starting Your Job Search

Internet Job Search

Blessed New Business Start-up

Working with Recruiters and Headhunters

Researching a Company

Dress for Success (Great First Impressions)

Interviewing and Thank You Letters

Networking and Informational Interviews

Creating a Powerful Résumé and Cover Letter

Creating a Business Portfolio

Establishing Personal and Professional References

Salary Negotiating and Accepting Job Offers

Making Job Fairs Work for You

First Day on Your New Job

Goal Setting

Personal Financial Management

Action Planning for Your Personal life

Seminar Course Offerings

Finding Your Perfect Career
This seminar will reveal how to select a career that best fits your skills, interests, and purpose in the workplace.

Starting Your Job Search
You will learn about valuable resources to use during your job search. Some resources include job hotlines, Web sites, and recruiting agencies.

Looking for a Job on the Internet
Participants will learn basic Internet terms and become familiar with major recruiting resources on the World Wide Web.

Working with Recruiters & Job Headhunters
You will learn the difference between working with a recruiter and headhunter. Receive valuable documents to assist you in working with multiple sources.

Researching a Company
This seminar will reveal the proper steps and resources needed in researching a company.

Dress for Success (Great First Impressions)
Participants will learn the proper way to dress for a job interview.

Interviewing & Thank You Letters

This seminar will reveal the proper way to ask and respond to interview questions. Receive sample interview questions and letters to use during your job search.

Professional Networking & Informational Interviews

Identify 100 networking sources to use during your job search. Receive documents to assist you with your meetings.

Creating a Powerful Cover Letter & Résumé

Participants will learn about different résumé styles and determine the best one to use.

How to Create a Business Portfolio & Establish References

This seminar will show you how to create a business portfolio and identify the best way to request references.

Salary Research, Negotiating, and Accepting Job Offers

You will learn how to research salaries and feel confident while asking the interviewer for the proper salary pay range.

Making Job Fairs Work For You

Learn the proper way to work a job fair to ensure that your time is used effectively and efficiently.

First Day On Your New Job

Learn about what to cover daily, weekly, monthly, quarterly, and yearly with your supervisor on your new job.

What to Do If You Get Laid Off or Let Go

This seminar will reveal proper steps and resources to use after your employment ceases.

Job Shadowing

Participants will identify people that they would like to job shadow for a day. Receive valuable resources to assist you with your job shadowing experience.

Action Planning for Your Personal Life

This seminar will reveal proper steps to create an action plan for your personal and work related projects.

Goal Setting (Short-Term & Long-Term)

Participants will learn how to set short term and long term goals for their personal and professional life. Participants will complete two goals during the session.

How to Create Mission & Vision Statements

This seminar will reveal how to develop a mission and vision statement for your personal or professional life.

Personal Financial Management

This seminar will reveal steps to help improve your personal financial management skills. Participants will learn how to create and stick to a monthly budget, pay bills on time, respond to creditors, and much more!

Blessed New Business Start-up

In this workshop you will learn how to write out your God given business idea vision, make it plain and map it out upon tables so you can run with it!

FREE COVER LETTER & RÉSUMÉ EVALUATIONS

Your cover letter and résumé are the first impression that you may give a prospective employer. The purpose of both documents is to ultimately "get you the interview." It is very important that your cover letter and résumé look professional.

Have an experienced human resource professional review your cover letter and résumé before it is submitted to recruiters and employers. You can send your documents to "Be Blessed" Career Consulting Inc. to receive a FREE evaluation.

Your cover letter and résumé will be reviewed in detail by an experienced human resource professional. After both documents are reviewed, you will receive an overall evaluation, including valuable recommendations for next steps within two weeks of submission. We look forward to hearing from you.

Send Your Cover Letter and Résumé Today!

"Be Blessed" Career Consulting Inc.
Free Evaluation
P.O. Box 4373
Southfield, MI 48037

E-mail: beblessedcc@aol.com
Web site: www.BeBlessedCareerConsulting.co

OTHER RECOMMENDED BOOKS & REFERENCE MATERIAL

The following are other recommended books by Kimberly A. Benjamin of "Be Blessed" Career Consulting Inc:

How to Be Highly Favored and Empowered to Prosper in Your Job Search Workbook (ISBN # 0-9766785-1-9)

COMING SOON!

My Personalized 30 Day Job Search Plan
My Job Search Journal
My Job Search Prayer Book
and
"BE BLESSED" HOW TO POCKET GUIDES BOOK SERIES
How to Find a Perfect Career
How to Survive Getting Laid Off or Let Go
How to Start Your Job Search
How to Work with Recruiters and Headhunters
How to Research a Company for a Job Interview
How to Dress for Success
How to Improve Your Interviewing Skills
How to Improve Your Networking Skills
How to Create a Business Portfolio
How to Improve Your Salary Research and Negotiating Skills

How to Complete an Employment Application
How to Properly Accept a Job Offer
How to Make Job Fairs Work For You
How to Improve Your Goal Setting Skills
How to Set Short-term and Long-term Goals
How to Improve Your Money Management Skills

OTHER BOOKS

Finding and Fulfilling Your Purpose at Work
Dr. J. Victor and Catherine B. Eagan (ISBN 0-967-8889-2-1)
How to Discover Your Purpose in 10 Days:
God's Path to a Full and Satisfied Life
Dr. J. Victor and Catherine B. Eagan (ISBN 1-932477-00-4)
How to Discover Your Purpose in 10 Days Prayers and Daily Journal
Dr. J. Victor and Catherine B. Eagan
(ISBN 1-932477-01-2)
How to Discover Your Purpose in
10 Days Self Assessment Workbook
Dr. J. Victor and Catherine B. Eagan
(ISBN 1-932477-02-0)

ENDNOTES

Character Training Institute, Character Determines Success Pocket Guide, Character First 2004, s.v. "Diligence."

Random House Unabridged Dictionary, 1997, s.v. "Resourcefulness."

Character Training Institute, Character First Bulletins, 2002, s.v. "Self-Control."

Benard Haldane Associates, "8 Myths About Job Hunting," http://www.job-hunting.com (accessed April 7, 2005).

Webster's New Riverside Dictionary, 1996 , s.v. "Excellence."

Character Training Institute, Character Determines Success Pocket Guide, Character First, 2004, s.v. "Decisiveness."

Dr. J. Victor Eagan and Catherine B. Eagan, Finding and Fulfilling Your Purpose at Work, (Southfield, MI: Workplace Wisdom Publishing, 2002), pg. ix-x.

Dr. J. Victor Eagan and Catherine B. Eagan, Using the Resources of God to Succeed at Work, (Southfield, MI: Workplace Wisdom Publishing, 2000), pg. 2.

Yahoo Inc., Yahoo Home Page, http://www.yahoo.com (accessed April 7, 2005).

AltaVista USA, AltaVista Home Page, http://www.altavista.com (accessed April 7, 2005).

Google, Google Home Page, http://www.google.com(accessed April 7, 2005).

Fortune, Fortune.com Home Page, http://www.fortune.com (accessed April 7, 2005).

The American Heritage Dictionary English Language, 2000, s.v. "Patience."

Webster's II New Riverside Dictionary, 1996, s.v. "Meekness."

New Horizons Computer Learning Centers, New Horizons Home Page, http://www.newhorizons.com (accessed April 7, 2005)

Random House Unabridged Dictionary, 1997, s.v. "Faith"

Webster's II New Riverside Dictionary, 1996, s.v. "Peaceable"

Webster's II New Riverside Dictionary, 1996, s.v. "Gentle"

Random House Unabridged Dictionary, 1997, s.v. "Easy"

Random House Unabridged Dictionary, 1997, s.v. "Mercy"

Job Star, Job Star Home Page,http://www.jobstar.org (accessed April 7, 2005).

Career Builder, Career Builder Home Page,http://www.careerbuilder.com (accessed April 7, 2005).

Career Services and Placement, CSP Home Page,http://csp.msu.edu/cdd/career (accessed April 7, 2005).

Monster, MonsterTrack Home Page,http://www.monstertrak.com (accessed April 7, 2005).

WetFeet, WetFeet Home Page, http://www.wetfeet.com (accessed April 7, 2005).

Society of Human Resource Management, SHRM Home Page,

http://www.shrm.org (accessed April 7, 2005).

HotJobs, HotJobs Home Page,http://www.hotjobs.com (accessed April 7, 2005).

Wageweb, Wageweb Home Page, http://www.wageweb.com (accessed April 7, 2005).

Recourse Communications Inc., BestjobsUSA Home Page, http://www.bestjobsusa.com (accessed April 7, 2005).

Abbott Langer & Associates Inc., Abbott Langer & Associates Home Page, http://www.abbott-langer.com (accessed April 7, 2005).

US Department of Labor, Bls.gov Home Page, http://stats.bls.gov (accessed April 7, 2005).

Jack Chapman, How to Make 1000 a Minute, (Boulder, CO: Career Track Inc., 1998).

Minister Armand Dabney, Minister Nancy Dabney and Minister Joyce Burton, I AM Scriptures Handout, Word of Faith International Christian Center, 2004.

Be Blessed Career Consulting Inc., Be Blessed Career Consulting Inc. Home Page, http://www.BeBlessedCareerConsulting.com (accessed April 7, 2005).

If This Book Has Changed Your Life,
We Want to Hear From You!

CONTACT US TODAY AT:

"Be Blessed" Career Consulting Inc.

P.O. Box 4373 Southfield, MI 48037

E-mail: Beblessedcc@aol.com

Phone: (586) 718-2571

www.BeBlessedCareerConsulting.com